1400 Ideas
for Speakers
and Toastmasters

Herbert V. Prochnow

Baker Books

A Division of Baker Book House Co
Grand Rapids, Michigan 49516

Reprinted 1970, 1994 by Baker Books
a division of Baker Book House Company
P.O. Box 6287, Grand Rapids, MI 49516-6287

Printed in the United States of America

ISBN 0-8010-7143-7

CONTENTS

PREFACE

There are in this book 1400 humorous stories, epigrams, witticisms, unusual facts and illustrations, stories of persons and events, selections from speeches and other sources, quotations from the Bible and from literature, and unusual comments from modern sources.

These hundreds of items can be used in speeches, introductions by toastmasters, and in conversation. The book is intended to be a practical reference volume which may be used many times. The general reader may also find in these items, many stories, illustrations, witticisms and quotations of interest to him.

In Chapter 1, there are some concise statements of the responsibilities of both the speaker and the toastmaster. These may help to make clear the precise responsibilities these persons have. There are tens of thousands of meetings each year and the contribution which competent speakers and efficient chairmen and toastmasters can make to assure worthwhile meetings for literally millions of persons is very great. One meeting of 100 persons lasting only one hour is equal to 100 hours of time consumed. Any preparation and thought which can be taken to assure better meetings can do immeasurable good.

If this reference book makes even a modest contribution to more interesting and worthwhile meetings and to better introductions, it will have served its objective in a field where there is a real opportunity for improvement.

Herbert V. Prochnow

CHAPTER I

THE SPEAKER'S AND TOASTMASTER'S RESPONSIBILITIES

The reader will find in this chapter a concise statement in outline form of the responsibilities of both the speaker and the toastmaster. In the chapters which follow there are 1400 humorous stories, witticisms, quotations, illustrations from famous lives and examples that may be used in the preparation of the speaker's and toastmaster's remarks.

You can speak with confidence if you speak on a subject in which you are competent and to which you give thorough and complete preparation. Then you will be better informed on the subject than most members of your audience. You can use the hundreds of items in this book in speeches to clarify and emphasize your points and to make your comments interesting.

THE SPEAKER'S RESPONSIBILITY

1. No one should ever accept an invitation to speak unless the preparation he has made or expects to make will assure a worthwhile message.

2. It is not enough to enunciate well and to speak clearly. A speaker's primary responsibility is to have the audience feel that the time spent was worthwhile. Most of us are not humorists or comedians. We are not entertainers. This means therefore that it is necessary for a speaker to make some contribution to the thinking of the members of the audience. And this is not easy. It requires hard work and study to make a thoughtful speech.

3. No speaker should agree to speak on a subject regarding which he is not really competent.

4. Proper preparation requires that the speaker make at least a written outline of a speech. This helps to assure that the speaker himself clearly recognizes the major points he wishes to make and has arranged his material in logical and convincing order.

5. The major idea that is to be presented may generally be divided into two, three or four points. As a rule four is the maximum number. These points must be closely related to the major idea.

6. It is not necessary to write out a speech fully. However, the author of this book invariably writes out his speeches and refines the language almost to the moment when the speech is actually delivered. Writing the speech and refining it is a desirable discipline. It eliminates all unrelated ideas and all unnecessary words. The speaker may finally speak from an outline but he has first thought through and set down his ideas clearly and logically. The author writes his speeches out fully, and refines and tightens the language. He does not read a speech but has it before him on 5 x 8 cards as he speaks. The cards are marked to indicate any parts that may need to be omitted if time should unexpectedly require shortening the remarks. A speaker should be ready for this kind of emergency.

7. Refining a speech takes various forms. Unnecessary words or phrases are eliminated. An epigram or witticism may be inserted to bring out a point. To lend emphasis, a short sentence of only three or four words will be inserted after several longer sentences. A pertinent quotation from literature may be added at an appropriate place. An example, illustration, or statistics may be included to make a point clear.

8. Most speakers will probably find it desirable to divide a speech into three parts: the introduction; the body of the address; and the conclusion. The introduction indicates the subject to be discussed and may give background for the discussion. The body of the address contains the two, three or four points to be made. The conclusion should be short and should summarize the points made or state the conclusion that follows from the remarks made. It may call for some specific action. By use of a Biblical quotation, a story, or an unusual example it may bring the address to a dramatic conclusion.

9. When the speaker has given what obviously is his conclusion, he must not give another conclusion. With an attentive audience, a speaker may be tempted to restate his conclusion with the hope that he can further emphasize what

he tried to say. This is a serious mistake. One should make the best conclusion possible and then stop.

10.   There are a few other matters that must be kept in mind.

A.   Find out how much time you are to be given for your speech and observe this limitation.

B.   Unless some unusual development requires a change, adhere closely to the address you have prepared. If you depart from the speech you had thoughtfully prepared, you may omit the points you intended to make, you may become wordy, and you may run over your time as you pursue ideas that suddenly occur to you. Briefly, the danger is that you will ramble.

C.   Go over your prepared speech often enough so you are thoroughly familiar with it. No audience wants to hear a speaker practice with material with which he is not familiar.

D.   Speak sufficiently loud to be heard. If a microphone is used, be careful not to turn so far from it that your voice fades out. Speak in to the microphone.

E.   It is generally wise not to speak to an audience on a subject in which the audience is apt to have little or no interest.

THE TOASTMASTER'S RESPONSIBILITIES

1.   Make certain that the program deals with a subject of importance and of interest to the audience.

2.   Choose a speaker with the greatest care, for the responsibility for the success of the meeting clearly rests upon you. You must be as certain as possible that the speaker you choose will deliver a worthwhile address. This is the reason you chose him.

3.   Make certain that the speaker understands the character of the audience, the subject he is expected to discuss, the date and the place. You may also wish to make hotel reservations for him and meet his plane or train.

4.   All the details such as the luncheon or dinner menu, the ventilation of the room, the physical comfort of the audience, the precise time schedule for each part of the meeting, the reception of the speaker, announcements during the meeting, the podium, the loudspeaker, and the seating arrangements at the speaker's table are your responsibility.

5. Your remarks should be fully prepared in advance. You should have gone over them often enough to have them clearly in mind.

6. If the occasion permits, it is desirable to have at least a little humor in your remarks as chairman.

7. You will need to remember also that the speaker is making the speech and you are introducing him. Not all chairmen are aware of the difference. Your comments should fit into the time schedule precisely.

8. The introduction should be good and lead the audience to believe that they are fortunate to have the speaker. However, the remarks should not be so extravagant that they embarrass the speaker or make it impossible for him to live up to the remarks made. No speaker is a combination of Demosthenes, Socrates, Jefferson and Lincoln.

9. After the speaker completes his address, express appreciation to the audience for his presentation.

10. If the organization has no funds for an honorarium, it is nevertheless desirable if some small gift can be given as a token of appreciation for the speech. Any speaker who makes a worthwhile address must give much time and thought to it.

11. If publicity is desired the press should be given all the facts regarding the meeting. The speaker may be willing to give you a copy of his remarks for the press. In addition, you may arrange an interview for the speaker with the press, assuming the press desires it and the speaker is willing. A special table for the press at the luncheon or dinner is often helpful in giving the meeting wide publicity. Most speakers are willing to provide photographs and at least excerpts of their remarks for publicity.

12. If there are radio and television stations in the community, you may be able to arrange for them to use portions or even all the remarks of the speaker. It is advisable always to advise the speaker in advance of such arrangements to be certain that he has no objections.

THE SECRET OF SUCCESS

The secret of success in making a speech or in acting as a toastmaster is in the preparation. One must prepare and prepare and prepare. Confidence then comes naturally.

CHAPTER II

EPIGRAMS, WITTICISMS AND QUIPS

Most of us can stand adversity but prosperity is another matter.

One thing comes to the man who waits, and that's whiskers.

Your best friends are generally those you don't meet very often.

If you are ready to give someone a piece of your mind, be sure you can get along on what you have left.

Some persons speak wise words in fun but a good many others speak foolish words in earnest.

Most ideas are not unusual but the experience of having ideas is unusual.

Nothing is further than the distance between advice and help.

If ignorance is bliss most of us should be very happy.

Years make all of us old and very few of us wise.

In modern education children learn how to spell a word at least two ways.

He who laughs last must have time to waste.

A woman never makes a fool of a man, but she sometimes helps direct the performance.

The person who tells you his troubles keeps you from talking about yours.

Some persons who are too proud to beg and too honest to steal, borrow and forget to pay.

If you know you don't know much, you know more than most people.

A thoughful wife has some steaks in the freezer when her husband returns from a fishing trip.

A satellite is an employee at a party the boss gives.

All you need in life is a comfortable bed and comfortable shoes because you are in one or the other all your life.

If you say you are less wise than you are, people will think you are wiser than you are.

In the United States a boy can grow up and hope to be

President, but in Soviet Russia he only hopes to grow up.

Juvenile delinquents are alike in too many disrespects.

A good idea can get very lonely in an empty head.

No matter how much money talks most people don't find it boring.

You may have a high opinion of yourself and still rate pretty low.

Anyone can be a fool in so many ways it's hard to avoid all of them.

Good conduct deserves commendation, but it isn't easy to become famous for it.

What the United States does not need is a five cent dollar.

No horse goes as fast as the money you bet on him.

A telephone isn't a vacuum cleaner but some people can get a lot of dirt out of it.

When you buy something for a song, the accompaniment is probably expensive.

A spendthrift is a person who tries to get more out of life than there is in it.

A fall guy is any member of a Latin American cabinet.

An honest wife is one who lies only about her age, weight and her husband's salary.

No opportunity is lost; the other fellow takes it.

What this country needs is an electric blanket that pops you out of bed like a toaster.

Nothing makes you feel better off than your first ride on a horse.

If you want to know where you can spend your vacation, read your checkbook.

What some persons seem to want is a five-day weekend.

The family that isn't in debt today is underprivileged.

Success in life is being able to afford spending what you are already spending.

What will today's children be able to tell their children they had to do without?

Good manners consist in letting others tell you what you already know.

Some persons pay their bills when due, some when overdue and some never do.

There has been only one indispensable man and that was Adam.

There are always some persons who are willing to neglect

their work in order to tell you how to run your affairs.

Nothing is easier than getting up early in the morning the night before.

Some folks speak when they think, and some oftener.

No woman likes a perfect husband, because it doesn't give her anything to do.

Nothing beats a wastebasket as a labor-saving device.

No one worries now about the wolf at the door as long as you can feed him on the instalment plan.

If a man tries as hard to keep his wife after marriage as he tried to get her, they will get along well.

All things come to him who goes down a one-way street in the wrong direction.

The way to win friends is to lose arguments.

Poverty is not a disgrace, but that's its one advantage.

A smart wife will back up her husband in an argument — up against the wall.

If the months were made shorter we wouldn't have so much month left over at the end of the money.

You never need to do over a job you did well, unless it's weeding the garden.

The way to a man's heart, and also his pocketbook, is through his hobby.

Sometimes a person may be more quiet because he has more to be quiet about.

The fellow who puts on the dog often puts off the creditors.

Don't worry about what people think of you because they seldom do.

Many of us believe that wrong isn't wrong if it's done by nice people like ourselves.

An economist is a person who explains later how the things he didn't expect were inevitable.

When you go on a vacation to forget everything, you generally find when you open your bag at the hotel that you have.

Some people grin and bear it — others buy and charge it.

A dollar goes a lot further if it is accompanied by some sense.

Opportunities drop in your lap if you have your lap where opportunities drop.

If you sing when you are sad, others can be sad with you.

If things are going too well, you are probably going downhill.

In an argument a person is tactful when he says "I couldn't possibly fail to disagree with you less".

Money doesn't make you happy but it helps to soothe your nerves.

When a person slaps you on the back, he does it to help you swallow what he is telling you.

The person who shouts the loudest for justice generally means in his favor.

A person with a million dollars may be a bad egg, but he generally gets by pretty well until he is broke.

One of the first things man learns is to talk, and later in life he learns to keep still.

As the attractive young lady said, "a man without a country is bad but a country without a man is worse".

Sometimes it isn't easy to tell whether it is opportunity or temptation knocking.

In a communist country a man can talk his head off very easily.

The young man who drives with one arm will either walk down or be carried up a church aisle.

Wisdom on the part of a wife is to let her husband have her way.

No two women are alike and neither is any one woman.

The way to be successful is to follow the advice you give others.

Little things keep one awake at night, especially those from three to six months of age.

Man needs but little here but dough.

Marriage is a mutual partnership with the husband mute.

In public libraries, except in Boston, low conversation is permitted.

Why is it that the other fellow always thinks he is carrying the load when we know we are.

The way to keep closets clean is to get a bigger garage.

In some cities a thief who breaks into the city hall can steal the results of the next election.

Time is a great healer but it's not much of a beauty parlor.

One way to get rid of weight is to leave it on the plate.

If the world was created out of chaos, we're now back about where we started.

If you begin to wonder something is worth what is costs, you are getting old.

Every now and then you have to applaud even the brighest child with one hand.

A small man behind a big title is sometimes as ferocious as a small dog behind a big fence.

Every young girl looks forward to the bride side of life.

Most pepole today never stay long enough in one place to get homesick when they leave.

When you get to the top of the long ladder of success, remember that it took a good many people to hold the ladder.

No secret is harder to keep than your opinion of yourself.

The earth revolves on its axis but the nations revolve on their taxes.

Sympathizing with some persons is like patting a dog on the head — they both follow you around for more.

It is unfortunate that many citizens demand something for nothing and even more unfortunate that they get it.

The man who is willing to make a fool of himself generally succeeds.

You don't get rid of your temper when you lose it.

When you make a fool of yourself, it isn't so bad if you know who did it.

When a thought strikes a person, no one can tell what will happen.

A secret is either not worth keeping or too good to keep.

The fellow who has a million dollars doesn't need to worry about his grammar.

It is hard to be happy if you do not have enough and it's impossible if you have too much.

Too many persons are short on horsepower and long on exhaust.

The main difference between death and taxes is that taxes get worse every time Congress meets.

The person who hears on radio and TV all the things wrong with him is lucky he feels as well as he does.

Parrots don't know what they are talking about and that makes them almost human.

Don't expect too much of another person because he is about like you and me.

Science provides many benefits, but it has never been able to make men love their neighbors.

Some persons are able to recognize their duty in time to sidestep it.

When father is on the day shift and mother is on the club shift, the children shift for themselves.

The person who is always harping on something isn't necessarily an angel.

Some persons get very tired overcoming obstacles before they come to them.

Wise words are sometimes spoken in jest, but foolish ones are often spoken in earnest.

The person who has nothing to say often proves it.

Money doesn't bring happiness but it enables you to choose some very pleasant misery.

Most of us can't stand prosperity and most of us don't have to.

If absence makes the heart grow fonder, some persons are in love with the church.

No two persons are alike, and this makes it possible for each of us to be conceited.

"I think" is an over-worked expression and almost always a gross exaggeration.

When day is done so is the average mother or father.

Time flits when you pay the youngster who baby sits.

The most difficult meal for a wife to get is breakfast in bed.

It's not at his mother's knees but across them where a youngster learns his best lessons.

A fool and his money can throw a lot of parties.

Travel doesn't broaden you as much as all the food you eat traveling.

Vacation is the period when you spend two weeks in an old shack without conveniences so you go back to your home with its comforts and complain.

The communist nations have less than we have and they want to share it with us.

The person who picks a tough job won't have much competition.

A politician who does nothing but keep his ear to the ground doesn't have much vision.

Every dog has his day but the road hog takes Sunday afternoon.

When you visit a modern art gallary you realize things are never as bad as they are painted.

You can fool all people some of the time but you can fool yourself all the time.

The fellow who lives in a house by the side of the road and watches the world go by now is in a trailer.

In the average family she is the treasure and he is the treasury.

How do you start a conversation in Hawaii where the weather is the same all the year around?

From the standpoint of education you can get a lot of first-hand knowledge from a second-hand car.

Did you ever notice how nice you can be to someone you think can do you a favor?

Some persons live by the Golden Rule and others settle for brass.

If you are right, what's the use of arguing, and if you are wrong what's the use?

Money talks but it doesn't hear well when you ask it to stay with you longer.

A pessimist is a person who knows himself and doesn't like what he finds.

One thing you have to say for many modern women is that they aren't effeminate.

Man is the only animal that laughs and has a state legislature.

Loneliness is the feeling you have when you are without money among relatives.

The part of a woman's work that is never done is what she asked her husband to do.

You seldom are so busy that you can't stop and tell others how busy you are.

No one has as many relatives as the fellow who makes a million dollars.

Any game in which you hold hands is generaly expensive.

Most of us believe we are as good as we never were.

Nothing is better for youngsters than some loving discipline.

When the boss has an idea you either see the light or feel the heat.

The average family could spend more money than it earns and generally does.

We like the housewife who knows what to do with leftovers — throw them out.

Half the world is always ready to tell the other half how to live.

Some people will roll out the red carpet for you today and pull it out from under you tomorrow.

A man who puts on a million airs seldom becomes a millionaire.

We know about how many blondes and brunettes there are in the country, but we have no record of the number of blockheads.

This country has some fine old ruins, but you have to go to a night club to see them.

It's surprising how many persons will agree with you if you keep your mouth shut.

To get ahead you have to tell your dollars where to go instead of asking them where they went.

Aren't there times in your life when you would rather have a lie told about you than the truth?

Remember the old days when the automobile windshield didn't have so many stickers you could look through it.

A person may be as young as he feels, but he is not often as important.

There is no use in worring about your old troubles when you know new ones will be coming along.

A human being is the only animal that can be skinned more than once.

He is the kind of do-it-yourself person who hits the nail right on the thumb.

One thing most nations have learned is that buying wars on the deferred payment plan is expensive.

Most women want a permanent wave but most men would like permanent hair.

You can't mind your own business if you haven't any mind and any business.

It's bad manners to talk when your mouth is full or your head is empty.

We sort of like the person who is dumb but keeps it to himself.

Why is it that what you hear is always less interesting than what you overhear.

The one comforting thing about an economist is that no one else can predict the future either.

Never bet on a sure stock market tip unless you can afford to lose.

As Baron Rothschild is reported to have said, "To make a fortune you must buy low and sell too soon."

Unfortunately, all the dummies in the movies aren't thrown over the cliff.

Perhaps the reason we have juvenile delinquency is that we don't have enough stern punishment.

Some people would rather be wrong in an argument than quiet.

If you try to get something for nothing, you must be certain you don't end up getting nothing for something.

The way to get in "Who's Who" is to know What's What.

Some persons are so unlucky they don't recognize their duty in time to sidestep it.

The person who frequently is tight as a drum is seldom fit as a fiddle.

When some women promise to be on time, it carries a lot of wait.

One comfort is that when you lose $5 now you don't lose as much as you used to.

No one of us is useless so long as he can serve as a horrible example.

People who live in glass houses have to answer the doorbell.

The way to kill time profitably is to work it to death.

If you think money grows on trees, sooner or later you will get caught out on a limb.

The hardest dollar to earn is the one you have already spent.

Some people are the life of the party, after they leave.

One thing that keeps some people from having a nervous breakdown is that they can't afford it.

Nothing is easy in the world except spending money.

The average is the poorest of the good and the best of the bad.

A great man makes some mistakes, but he is greater than the mistakes he makes.

After all is said and done, the wife has said it and the husband has done it.

The UN diplomats should probably be paid on a peace-work basis.

The only substitute for work is a miracle.

Nothing is opened by mistake more often than the mouth.

A husband's views are not necessarily those of the management.

A scientist described life as the metabolic activity of protoplasm, and sometimes it seems even worse.

When you cross the International date line you lose a day but you can do better than that if you cross the line on a busy highway.

Occasionally you meet a person who thinks that if he hadn't been born people would wonder why.

With a load of instalment payments the Joneses probably have a tough time keeping up with themselves.

All things come to him who waits, but not soon enough to do any good.

It's hard to believe that someone can differ with us and be right.

Success is relative, and the more you have of it the more relatives.

If a man has a wife who tells him what to do and a secretary who does it he may be a success.

Most women stay pretty as they grow older but it takes a little longer.

If you want a knot on your head, put a chip on your shoulder.

None but the brave can afford the fair.

Some persons never appeal to God unless they are getting licked.

If every mischievous youngster was sure of getting his reward in the end, we might do away with juvenile delinquency.

The news from over the world is sometimes bad and sometimes even worse.

It's sad to have loved and lost, but it is cheaper.

Politician's Re-election Slogan: Honesty is no substitute for experience.

To win an argument one must always argue with someone who knows less than he does, but that isn't easy either.

We have seen some women who have discovered the secret of perpetual emotion.

Equality means every one is as good as everyone else, and generally better.

A woman doesn't have to be musical to get airs out of a mink coat.

Man is superior because of all the animals only he survives the cruelty and greed of man.

A medical specialist is a man who wants all your teeth pulled before he tries another guess.

Nothing holds back progress like ignorance which is confident, and if it is enthusiastic also, it's unbeatable.

Some married couples don't get along because they have nothing in common to quarrel about.

Our idea of a fine job for a fellow who is tired of living is that of Secretary of Agriculture.

It's almost impossible for a statesman to be right without being too unpopular to be elected.

It takes three generations to make a gentleman because most of us only work at it part time.

Walking has some merit because it does get you out to the garage.

The less you know, the easier it is to be certain.

An automobile is only as sober as the driver.

The person who agrees with everything you say probably isn't worth talking to.

We don't know where this generation is going, but it isn't losing any time getting there.

Tomorow may never come but the morning after always does.

Many people now use the sign language. They sign for this and sign for that.

Some men are like whales — when they get to the top they blow.

The way to pass a twenty ton truck on a two lane highway is on a parallel road in the next county.

Figures don't lie, and that't exactly what makes tailoring so difficult.

Does a two car instalment buyer pay on one car one month and the other car the next?

Every man likes a woman with brains enough to tell him how wonderful he is.

No wonder children are confused when we tell them they're too little to stay up at night and too big to stay in bed in the morning.

Jet planes fly faster than sound, but we still think time flies fastest of all.

Two can drive worse than one.

Americans sink millions of dollars in unsound financial schemes, one of which is keeping up with the neighbors.

Every day the rest of the world gets nearer and dearer to us.

Some of the backward nations sometimes seem very forward.

By the time this country exhausts all its gasoline, there will be so many cars they can't move anyhow.

If you think of the things you don't have and don't want, you'll find you're pretty rich.

It is strange why other people do not profit when we point out their mistakes.

The more arguments you win, the fewer friends you have.

Why are the ignorant always so certain and the intelligent so uncertain.

He was the kind of cautious person who thought things over carefully before going off half-cocked.

No boy expects to grow up and be as dumb as his father.

A good listener usually dozes or has his mind on something else.

The boss may not be able to make you do anything, but he can make you wish you had.

A person ought to be thankful when he has the means to live beyond.

The thing that puzzles us is why the things we don't want are always cheaper.

One half the world is ignorant of how the other half lives, but that isn't true in the consumer loan departments.

In an election year, remember they also serve who only stand and vote.

The time when the fish bite is just before you get there and right after you leave.

No small boy can understand why grown-ups are asked to judge jam and jelly exhibits at the country fairs.

One thing is certain — you never get lonely at the bottom of the ladder.

It's not always easy to get the rising generation up in the morning.

Love makes the world go round but it doesn't have the same effect on a $40 a week salary.

A man with a good memory must worry about a lot of things he would like to forget.

We notice that the women's dress and millinary shops all have expensive lounges where the women can rest while the fashions change.

Nowadays the governments are occupied mainly with playing both ends against the taxpayer.

You don't have to be a magician to turn a conversation into an argument.

The School of Experience has no graduates, no degrees, and no survivors.

The person who longs for the good old days when you could get a pound of beef for 25 cents forgets that he worked an hour for it.

With winter here, we remember the little girl who defined "unaware" as what you put on first and take off last.

A maid disappeared with $6,000. Probably her pay-day.

If instalment terms get any longer, we'll need cars and TV sets that last as long as the instalment contract.

The number of revolutions in some countries is almost as absurd as the number of strikes we have here.

At home a person leaves more on the plate than he gets served in some high priced restaurants.

The trouble with farming as an occupation is that soil rhymes with toil.

The laborer is worthy of his hire. His labor should also be.

The person who is pleasure bent not only winds up bent, but broke.

One good thing about growing old is that you don't have to go to picnics.

Nothing is impossible. Now we have peace on a war basis.

Advice to the lovelorn is the bunk. If you're in love, you won't want it — or need it.

The desire for fame is simply the desire to write your own epitaph.

Sometimes we long for the good old days when all this country had to fear was an attack from the Indians.

Under a planned economy the government encourages the farmers to raise a bumper crop so the government will have to buy a lot of the bumper crop to keep from having a bumper crop.

Good judgment comes from experience and experience comes from poor judgment.

When you have trouble, you learn which friends have been waiting with a paddle to find you bent over.

To be frank is to tell the truth about anything that won't hurt you.

The greatest disadvantage in life is to have too many advantages.

Most persons who get something for nothing are disappointed if they don't get more.

We are not certain whether people are getting worse or whether the newspapers keep us better informed.

When you criticise your child for not being smart, remember a wooden head is one thing that can be inherited.

Husbands are said to be more honest than bachelors. They have to be.

Man reaps what he sows unless he is an amateur gardener.

Narrow-minded people are a nuisance if you find your conscience agrees with what they say.

Many a man tumbles over his own bluff.

The person who offers us advice for our own good seldom does us any.

When you say you will do a job tomorrow, ask yourself what you did about it yesterday.

People who offer good advice always offer it in the big economy size.

At international conferences we never seem to have any record of the still small voice.

Most of us are willing to follow the advice of our superiors if we can find any.

A bachelor is a fellow who can take a nap on top of a bedspread.

CHAPTER III

HUMOROUS STORIES AND COMMENTS
FOR ALL OCCASIONS

SCARED

My wife was in a minor auto bump, but she did sustain a cracked rib or two. She hadn't been to church for some time so she appeared the following Sunday. After the service the minister was shaking hands at the front door with members of the congregation when he saw her coming down the aisle. His face wrinkled into a broad grin and he said: "Scared you, didn't it?"

DON'T WORRY

"Why didn't you stop when I blew my whistle?" demanded the cop.

"I'm a little deaf," the lady driver explained apologetically.

"Well, don't worry," the officer reassured her. "You'll get your hearing tomorrow."

WHO? ME?

The personnel manager turned to the young man seeking a job. "Tell me," he said, "what have you done?"

"Me?" answered the startled applicant. "About what?"

WE HAVE

Any time you get to thinking how hard it is to meet new people, just pick up the wrong golf ball.

THAT WILL HOLD HIM

A car screeched to a halt at an intersection, barely missing a whitehaired old lady. But instead of giving the driver a tongue-lashing, she recovered herself quickly, smiled sweetly, and pointed to a pair of baby shoes dangling from his rearview mirror.

"Young man," she asked, "why don't you put your shoes back on?"

COMFORTING

A man accidentally swallowed a pingpong ball and he was rushed into surgery for its removal. The patient insisted on having only a local anaesthetic so he could watch the operation. He winced a little when the first incision was made, but he didn't actually feel it; nor did he feel the next cut, nor the next. However, he became a little alarmed at the number of incisions, as the surgeon cut here and there, in what seemed a rather random fashion.

"Why do you have to cut in so many places?" he asked.

"Well," replied the surgeon, cutting away, "that's the way the ball bounces!"

CORRECT

To make a long story short, there's nothing like having the boss walk in.

MISTAKE

An office worker, loafing at the breakfast table and leisurely reading the newspaper, asked his wife for another cup of coffee.

"Another cup?" asked his wife. "Aren't you gonig to the office today?"

"For Heaven's sake!" he exclaimed. "I thought I was at the office!"

HE LEARNED 'EM

Mother: "What did Mama's little boy learn in school today?"

Son: "I learned two other kids not to call me 'Mama's little boy.'"

WE AGREE

How nice it would be if all dieters would simply eat the calories allowed and not count the calories aloud.

GOOD BEGINNING

A doctor advised a woman that her husband required aboslute rest.

"Well, doctor," she continued, "he simply won't listen to me."

"A very good beginning, ma'am, a very good beginning," the doctor replied.

THAT'S DIFFERENT

"What do you mean you need a new car?" asked the father visiting his son at college. "Look at those old cars in the parking lot."

"But, Dad," the boy said, "those belong to the faculty."

WORTH REMEMBERING

He stopped griping when his boss sent him this memo: "Be thankful for problems, for if we didn't have them, you wouldn't be here; and if they were less difficult, someone with less ability would have your job."

IT COULDN'T

The scoffers said it couldn't be done, and the odds were so great, who wouldn't? But I tackled the job that couldn't be done, and what do you know! It couldn't!

BE CAREFUL

Wife to disgruntled husband, just home from work: "Judging by the expression on your face, I'd guess the people in your office had a very hard day."

WE MISSED IT, TOO

The Sunday School teacher was trying to bring a lesson heavily upon the minds of the pupils. "I want you to look at this picture," she said. "It illustrates today's lesson. Lot was told to take his wife and daughters and flee out of Sodom. Here are Lot and his daughters with his wife, and Sodom in the background. What else do you see?"

A little boy from the back of the room said, "Where is the flea?"

HE DID HIS BEST

"Just what good have you done for humanity?" asked the judge, before sentencing the habitual pick-pocket.

"Well," replied the confirmed criminal, thoughtfully, "I've kept several detectives working regularly."

IS THAT FAIR?

Typist: "But, Professor, isn't this the same exam you gave last year?"

Professor: "Yes, but I've changed the answers."

AN AMATEUR PLAY

Ted: "Did the school play have a happy ending?"

Ned: "It sure did! Everybody was very happy when it was over!"

FUNNY WORLD

This is a funny world — its wonders never cease. Civilized people are at war, and savages are at peace!

HE ISN'T THE ONLY ONE

Two opposing political candidates were debating on a busy street corner, while a group of spectators listened.

"There are hundreds of ways of making money," challenged one, "but only one honest way."

"And what's that?" jeered the other.

"Ah ha!" exulted the first speaker. "I thought you wouldn't know!"

HUSH

The barber was amazed to get a tip from his new customer before he even climbed into the chair.

"You're the first customer to give me a tip before I give him any service," said the barber.

"That's not a tip," was the answer. "That's hush money."

REVEALING TEST

We are always impressed by the acumen of psychologists, especially as their knowledge is applied to take the guesswork out of personnel relations.

An industrialist recently enlisted a psychological expert to help him select a new secretary.

He was puzzled as the psychologist said to three job candidates, "How much is two and two? Write down the answer on this paper."

The first girl hastily wrote, "Four."

The second girl, suspecting a trick, wrote "Twenty-two."

The third girl answered: "It could be four or it could be twenty-two."

In the next room, the psychologist explained: "Now you see how revealing are the answers to a simple test. The first girl has a very conventional mind. The second girl has imagination. The third girl is both practical and imaginative. Now which one do you prefer?" he beamed.

"I'll take the pretty blonde," replied the employer.

EXPERT

An expert is someone who is called in at the last minute to share the blame.

WHY?

We understand that a patient on a trip to Hawaii, cabled his psychiatrist: "Having a wonderful time. Why?"

A COMMON TECHNIQUE

There was a young 'cellist named Leo,
Who played in a Beethoven trio,
His technique was scanty
So he played it Andante
Instead of Allegro Con Brio.

HARD JOB

A Texas psychiatrist is said to be lecturing to PTA groups in Texas on the subject: "Alaska: How to explain it to your child."

WE ARE PLEASED TO INTRODUCE

Every rose has its thorn
There's fuzz on all the peaches.
There never was a dinner yet
Without some lengthy speeches.

HARD WORK

Kids have it tough. Where they used to walk to school and keep warm by running part of the way, now they stand and shiver waiting for the bus.

WE DOUBT IT

A speaker became the hit of the evening by honestly saying: "I'm speaking to you because I have nothing else to do — and I'm sitting down because I have nothing else to say."

THE DIFFERENCE

A psychotic builds castles in the air, a neurotic lives in them, but the psychiatrist collects the rent.

NEGLECTED

If you feel neglected, think of Whistler's father.

ONE TEST

Good breeding is that quality that enables a person to wait in well-mannered silence while the loud mouth gets the services.

JUST TRY IT

If you want the world to beat a path to your door, just lie down some Sunday afternoon and try to take a nap.

HE SURE DIDN'T

An American tourist went to visit one of the monumental cathedrals and was watching a wedding party. He turned to a nearby Frenchman and asked: "Who is the groom?"

"Je ne sais pas," murmured the native.

A few hours later, in another section of the cathedral, the tourist came upon a funeral procession. Looking around, he was surprised to see the same native nearby.

"Who's dead?" he asked.

"Je ne sais pas," replied the native.

"Wow!" declared the tourist. "He didn't last long!"

INTERESTING IDEA

Many persons would like to do something for a living that doesn't involve work.

AN IDEA

What a woman needs is a purse with a zipper on the bottom so she can find things quickly.

MARRIAGE

Dish towel: An object that wipes the contented look from a married man's face.

BEING QUIET

It's only natural for older folks to be quiet. They have so much more to be quiet about.

ANNOYING

A woman motorist was heard to say, "The thing I don't like about parking a car is that noisy crash at the end."

ONE MISTAKE WRIGHT MADE

When J. Edward Day, postmaster general, spoke in Pittsburgh he recalled that a score or more years ago the late Architect Frank Lloyd Wright was called in as a consultant on city planning, looked Pittsburgh over and came up with the terse advice — "Abandon it."

HE PREFERS SECOND BEST

A salesman described his recent visits to his doctor, brought on by increasing nervousness.

"The best thing for you to do," advised the physician, "is to give up smoking, drinking, late hours, and rich foods."

"I do not feel," replied the salesman, "that I deserve the best. What is your second best solution?"

EXPERIENCE

Experience is what keeps a man who makes the same mistake twice from admitting it the third time around.

A SERIOUS BLUNDER

The worst blunder a husband can make is to forget his wife's birthday, but remember her age.

DOES EVERYTHING FOR YOU

A customer in a sporting goods department was outfitting himself for his first hunting trip.

He kept studying the compass and finally blurted out: "What's the mirror on this compass for?"

"Well," declared the clerk, "you just look in there and it will tell you who is lost."

"I'LL SAY THEY DO

You may not know when you're well off, but the Internal Revenue Department does.

THEY ALWAYS DO

Never tell a girl you are unworthy of her — she knew it before you did.

PROBLEM SOLVED

A friend reports he just solved the parking problem: "I bought a parked car."

THIS MADE THE TEACHER SICK

Teacher: "Can you give me a sentence with the word 'officiate in it?"

Pupil: "A man got sick from a fish he ate."

DIFFICULT QUESTION

Girl: Of course I can live on your salary, but what would you live on?

ECONOMY

With the steady increase in government payrollers, Washington observers are recalling a story, credited years ago to Fred Busbey when he was a member of the House. Busbey said an efficiency expert was checking a government bureau and came to an office where two young men were seated on opposite sides of a desk, neither occupied with work.

"What are your duties?" the expert asked one.

"I've been here six months and I haven't been given any duties," the man replied.

"And your duties?" the expert asked the other man.

"I, too, have been here six months and have been given no duties," he replied.

"Well, one of you must go," snapped the expert. "This is an obvious instance of duplication."

SATISFACTION

Next to being shot at and missed, life's biggest satisfaction is making the final payment on a new car.

THAT'S DIFFERENT

A little boy came home from school all excited because a beautiful white rabbit named Snowball, used in his nature study class, was to be given to the lucky child whose name was pulled from a hat the next day.

To take part in the drawing, each child had to bring a note from home saying his parents would let him keep the animal if he won it.

The thought of another pet to cope with unnerved Willie's mother, but rationalizing that the chances of losing were good, with 28 in the class, she gave Wilie the note.

That afternoon Willie rushed home, and wildly announced that Snowball was his.

"You mean that out of the whole class, you won the bunny?" his mother asked incredulously.

"Well, not 'zactly," Willie said. "I was the only one with a note!"

GOOD FOR A SMALL PLACE

Eastern visitor in a western village: "What a beautiful sunset!"

Native: "Yeah, not bad at all for a little place like this."

A MAN

He wrecked his car, he lost his job, and yet throughout his life he took his troubles like a man — he blamed them on his wife.

BE CAREFUL

Little Johnny was in one of his very bad and disobedient moods. In answer to his mother's remonstrations that he behave himeself, he said: "Give me a nickel, and I'll be good."

"Give you a nickel!" she scolded. "Why, Johnny, you shouldn't be good for a nickel, you should be good for nothing — like your father."

NOT SO DUMB

The psychiatrist was testing the mentality of his patient. "Do you ever hear voices without being able to tell who is speaking, or where the voices come from?" he asked.

"Yes, sir," the patient replied.

"And when does this occur?" questioned the doctor.

"When I answer the telephone."

NOT SO TIRING

The couple had just returned from a trip to the coast, and their neighbors asked about it.

"We drove 5,000 miles in two weeks," the husband said.

The neighbors were impressed. "Some driving! Did it tire you?"

"Well, actually," the husband said, "my wife did the driving."

"And you enjoyed the scenery?" asked the incredulous neighbor.

"Yes — that, and held the wheel."

EXACTLY

A lady phoned her television serviceman, and complained that something was wrong with her set. The serviceman asked her whether there were any visible symptoms.

"Well, the newscaster is on right now," replied the lady, "and he has a very long face."

"Ma'am," replied the serviceman, "if you had to report what's happening in the world these days, you'd have a long face, too!"

HOW'S THAT?

The husband came home one evening and gave his wife an insurance policy. "I've insured my life for $25,000," he said, "so that if anything should happen to me, you would be provided for."

"How nice and thoughtful of you!" beamed his wife. "Now you won't have to go to the doctor every time you feel ill, will you?"

THAT GOES FOR MOST OF US

A janitor in a big city bank was sweeping the floor after banking hours when a telephone rang on an officer's desk. He took the receiver and said, "Hello," whereupon an excited voice demanded, "I want to know what the Federal Reserve Bank discount rate is, what the prime rate is, and if all this foreign travelling is going to upset our currency."

"Mr.," said the confused janitor, "I told you all I know about the banking business when I said 'hello.' "

HE WON'T BE BACK

"Willy," said the office manager, "there will be a vacancy here soon, and I'm thinking of giving your twin brother the job."

"My twin brother?" exclaimed Willy.

"Yes, the one I saw watching the ball game yesterday while you were at your aunt's funeral," explained the manager.

"Oh—er—yes," said Willy, hesitantly, "I—I remember. I'll go and hunt him up."

"Good!" said the manager, "and don't come back till you have found him!"

A DIFFICULT QUESTION

No trait is more useful in life than the ability to laugh

at our own defects, just as Lincoln was able to make fun of his homeliness.

Once, during a debate, Douglass accused Lincoln of being two-faced, but the rail-splitter without hesitation calmly responded: "I leave it to my audience — if I had two faces, would I be wearing this one?"

NOT SO GOOD

A wealthy contractor liked to know all about the employees who toiled in his vast business. One day he came upon a new young man who was dexterously counting out a large wad of the firm's cash into pay envelopes.

"Where did you get your financial training young man?" he asked.

"Yale," replied the young man.

"Good, good!" exclaimed the contractor, being a staunch advocate of higher learning.

"What's your name?"

"Yackson."

THE BEST PRICE

An old lady stepped up to the ticket window in the railroad station and asked, "How much is a ticket to Cleveland?"

"That's ten dollars and 79 cents," replied the agent.

The old lady turned to the little girl beside her and said, "I guess we may as well buy our tickets here. I've asked at all these windows, and they are the same price everywhere."

STARS TOO

Hollander: "Our flag has three stripes — red, white, and blue. These colors are related to our income tax. We get red in the face when we talk about them. We get white when we get the bill. We pay until we're blue in the face."

American: "It's the same in our country, only we see stars, too."

ILLITERATE

Teacher's note on report card: "Your son excels in

initiative, group integration, responsiveness and activity participation. Now if he'd only learn to read and write!"

IT HELPED HIM

"I understand that you've been going to a psychiatrist. Do you think it has helped you?"

"Certainly it has. Only a few weeks ago when the phone rang, I was deathly afraid to answer it. And now I go right ahead and answer it whether it rings or not."

A SMALL LARGE

A bewildered Englishman wandered into an American drugstore and asked for a small tube of toothpaste. The druggist handed him a package marked "Large."

"I asked for a small tube."

"That's right, sir" was the answer. "It comes in three sizes — Large, Giant and Super. I gave you the small size — Large."

SAME MISTAKE

Brown: "Back to town again? I thought you were a ranchman."

Green: "You made the same mistake I did."

A HOPELESS GUY

A man, threatening to end it all, was perched atop a tall building in Dallas, Texas, and a policeman had made his way to the roof to try and persuade him not to jump.

"Think of your mother and father," pleaded the cop.

"Haven't any," rejoined the man.

"Think of your wife and family," admonished the officer.

"Ain't got none."

"Your girl friend, then," tried the policeman.

"Hate women!"

"All right — think of Robert E. Lee," as a last resort.

"Who's Robert E. Lee?" asked the man, somewhat interested.

"Jump, yah cotton-pickin' Yankee!"

CORRECT

"Show me a man who understands women and I'll show you a man who is mistaken."

TV RATINGS

Bob Hope, speaking about the investigation by Congress into the television rating system: "It all started when Huckleberry Hound topped the President's state of the Union address."

LOST INTEREST

An advertising man was fired because his ulcer healed. The boss thought he had lost interest in his work.

HUMAN

One of the newest electronic computers is so human it blames its mistakes on others.

THE OLD DAYS

One vacationer reports seeing this sign in a restaurant on his travels: "Pies like mother used to make before she took up cocktails, bridge and cigarettes."

THAT'S DIFFERENT

The personnel manager was interviewing a man for a job and was going through the usual questions.

"Are you a clock watcher?" he asked.

"Nah, I've never had an inside job. I'm a whistle listener."

AUTOMATION

Automation is a man's effort to make work so easy that women can do it all.

MANY WILL AGREE

Teacher: "Which two documents contributed greatly to the U. S. government?"

Johnny: Forms 1040 and 1040-A."

MODERN YOUTH

A teacher was telling her second graders about various things on the farm, including the fact that chickens grow from tiny, fluffy chicks to full-grown roosters and hens with a full quota of feathers.

"That's strange," one little boy interrupted her, "our chickens don't have feathers — they have plastic bags on them!"

TOO TRUE

There is a line on the ocean where you lose a day when you cross it. There's a line on most highways where you can do even better.

PREPARED

Two foreman were comparing notes. "Do all the boys in your plant drop their tools the moment the whistle blows?" asked one.

"No, not all," replied the other forlornly. "The more orderly ones have their tools put away before that time."

THAT WILL TEACH THE CAT!

A lady visiting an aquarium asked where she could get a live shark.

"What do you want with a live shark?" the attendant asked.

"Well," she explained, "the neighbor's cat has been eating my goldfish, and I want to teach it a lesson!"

CORRECT?

Teacher: "Johnny, give me a sentence containing the words, deduct, defeat, defense, and detail."

Johnny, after some thought: "Defeat of deduct gets over defense before detail."

A GOOD QUESTION

A Quaker put a sign on a vacant piece of ground next to his home: "I will give this to anyone who is really satisfied."

A wealthy farmer, as he rode by, read it. Stopping, he said: "Since my Quaker friend is going to give that lot away, I may as well have it as anyone else. I am rich, I have all I need, so I am able to qualify." He went up to the door and explained why he had come.

"And is thee really satisfied?" asked the Quaker.

"Yes, I have all I need, and am well satisfied."

"Friend", rejoined the Quaker, "if thee is satisfied, what does thee want with my lot?"

WHO IS HOLDING OUT

One chorus girl was talking to another backstage at the end of the performance.

"What's wrong with the leading lady?" asked the first. "She acts mad about something."

"She only got nine bouquets over the footlights," replied the other.

"Nine?" exclaimed the first. "That's pretty good, isn't it?"

"Yeah," drawled her friend, "but she paid for 10."

HELPFUL

Behind every sucessful man stands a woman telling him that he's wrong.

IT'S NOT GOOD TO THINK

At night before I sleep, I lie and think and think, and wonder why — why tables have legs and cannot walk, why pitchers have mouths and cannot talk, why needles have eyes and cannot wink, why pins have heads and cannot think. Why houses have wings and cannot fly, why flowers have beds and cannot lie, why clocks have hands and cannot write, why combs have teeth and cannot bite.

I think and think till I can't sleep, and have to start in counting sheep. *From The Young Soldier.*

NO EXTRA PARTS

Joe saw the train but didn't stop. They dragged his auto to the shop. It took only a week or two to make the car as good as new. But, though they hunted high and low, they found no extra parts for Joe!

INSTRUCTIONS

A suburban housewife came home from a party to find a slip attached to the doorknob, which read:

"Notice of Census Taker's call. Please leave your filled-out form between the front door and scream."

HE WORKS FAST

The old storekeeper, who also was the community postmaster, was a real student of psychology. He had no helper, and when he had to leave the store to meet the mail train, especially during the tourist season, he was tormented by the thought of losing sales of gas and soft drinks while he was gone. He solved the problem shrewdly by printing a sign which explained everything in his absence. It read, "Back in 15 minutes. Already been gone 10."

CYNICAL

A bank clerk had always had a cynical view of human nature. When one of the town's citizens forgot to take four dollars' worth of change he had coming, the clerk posted a sign at the entrance:

"Will the person who forgot to take his four dollars' change form a line in front of my window tomorow morning."

MAYBE IT'S MUTUAL

The hardest time to disguise your feelings is when you're putting a bunch of relatives on the train.

A STATEMENT

A businessman sought to borrow $100,000 from the bank. "That's a lot of money," said the bank president. "Can you give me a statement?"

"Yes," said the businessman. "I'm optimistic."

OPTIMISM

Surveying, even lightly, these aspects of our political economy, one can agree with the eminent French biologist who said he felt "very optimistic about the future of pessimism."   *Elliott V. Bell*

ADVICE

"My advice, sir," said the mechanic to the car owner, "is that you keep the oil and change the car."

PROUD

Wife to husband on way home from party: "I was so proud of you, honey, the way you stood your ground and yawned right back at them!"

ANOTHER MATTER

The boss called the new stenographer into his office. "Miss Gann," he said, "you are the best-looking girl we ever had working in this office."

A pleased look came into the girl's eyes.

"You dress well," the boss continued, "you have a nice voice, you make a good impression on the public, and your deportment is fine."

"Oh, thank you," she said. "Your compliments are very pleasing."

"Enjoy them to the fullest," returned the boss, "because we are now going to discuss your spelling, punctuation and typing."

A COMMON EXPERIENCE

A young minister had just delivered a sermon at a church to which he hoped to be called.

"How was your sermon?" his wife asked.

"Which one?" he responded. "The one I was going to give, the one I did give, or the one I delivered so brilliantly on the way home in the car?"

GENEROUS

A woman lost a valuable diamond ring and claimed the $1,000 insurance, which the insurance company duly paid.

A year later she found the ring and wrote to the insurance company, stating that as she had found the ring she did not think it fair that she should keep the money. Accordingly she was sending it as a donation to the Boy Scouts.

HE KNOWS

The man who gets into a cage with a dozen lions impresses everyone but a school-bus driver.

LOGIC

Little Marjorie: "You gave Janie the biggest piece of cake."

Mother: "But you see, dear, Janie is bigger than you."

Little Marjorie: "Yes, and she always will be if you keep giving her the biggest piece of cake."

DIRECTIONS

Boy Scout leader to troop: "Remember, men, if you're lost in the woods at night, get your bearings from the sky. A glow will indicate the nearest shopping center."

SMART BOY!

"Daddy, will you give me 50 cents?" asked young Joe.

"When I was your age," replied his father, "I asked for pennies."

"O.K., give me 50 pennies."

ONE WAY TO DO IT

A friend of ours who is fond of fishing and water sports was anxious to buy a boat, but his wife had decided they couldn't afford one. Arriving home one evening, he calmly announced that he had bought a boat. His wife unleashed her wrath in all its glory. When she finally quieted down a half hour later, he figured the worst was over — and went out and bought the boat.

SOUNDS LOGICAL

Why does a rooster crow early in the morning?
Because he can't get in a word after the hens get up.

DEFINITIONS

Skier: A person with a two track mind.
Hobby: Voluntary work.
Listening: Silent flattery.
Shoplifting: Free enterprise.
Spring cleaning: Rearranging dust.

Arnold Glasow

POLITICALLY

During House debate on the military pay bill, to which was added 34 million dollars more than recommended, Representative Charles S. Joelson (D., N. J.) was moved to poetry and said:

One day we favor spending,
The next — of debt we prate.
Altho it's irresponsible,
Politically it's great.

THAT MADE IT BETTER

Bessie Besser bought some butter, but she said this butter's bitter. If I put it in my batter it will make my batter bitter. So Bessie Besser bought a bit of better butter, and she put the better butter in her batter and it made her batter better.

WE AGREE

A woman was somewhat disturbed to find herself seated at the left of her host instead of at the right, where she thought she should have been. "I suppose," she said, "it isn't always easy for you to seat people in their proper places."

"Oh," replied the host, "I find that those who matter don't mind and those who mind don't matter."

RIGHT ANSWER

Teacher: "This makes five times I have punished you this week. Now, Tommy, what have you to say?"
Tommy: "Well, I'm glad it's Friday."

ONLY THING POSSIBLE

A rural young man wrote to his uncle in the city to inquire about moving there.

"Can I live a Christian life in the city on $15 a week?" he wrote in the letter.

To this his uncle replied, "That's the only thing you can do."

IN LIVING COLOR

A P columnist Cynthia Lowry reported the reaction of a 3-year old who, while visiting the Memphis zoo, saw her first peacock: "Look Mama, there's a living color!"

TROUBLE AHEAD

Joe: "Say, where did you happen to get that red lantern?"

Sam: "I just found it. Some careless jerk left it by a hole in the ground."

EASY CHOICE

The young couple had just finished going over their monthly bills and were down to the last two.

"Honey," said the husband, "we're practically broke. I don't know which to pay — the electric company or the doctor."

"Oh, the electric company, of course," answered his wife. "After all, the doctor can't shut off your blood."

BEWILDERED

Daniel Boone was once asked whether he had ever been lost on his long hunts through the wilderness. "No," he replied. "I never got lost. But I was once bewildered for three days."

OF COURSE

Behind every successful man there's a woman — who finally catches him.

IS THIS CRAZY?

He is crazy about his wife, and he worships the ground her father struck oil on.

HE KNEW HIS BUSINESS

A gunman appeared at the paymaster's window of a large plant and said, "Never mind the pay roll, Bud! Just hand over the welfare fund, the group insurance premiums, the pension fund, and all the withholding taxes."

A COMMITTEE

Fahey Flynn, radio commentator, defines a committee as, "the unable who have been asked by the unwilling to do the unnecessary."

FANATIC

A fanatic is one who can't change his mind and won't change the subject.   *Winston S. Churchill*

NO MORE HOTELS

Sales manager: "What's this big item listed on your expense account?"

Salesman: "Why, that's my hotel bill."

Sales manager: "Well, don't buy any more hotels."

THE REAL QUESTION

"I hear you have a boy in college. Is he going to become a doctor, an engineer, or a lawyer, perhaps?"

The slow, quizzical answer was: "That I do not know. Right now the big question is: is he going to become a sophomore?"

THEY NEEDED IT

A woman always attended church and after each sermon would remark, "My, they certainly did need the message this morning." One snowy Sunday morning she was the only one in the congregation. The minister delivered his message anyway. He walked with her to the door, where she said, "My, they certainly would have needed it if they would have been here."

BUSY

She and her husband were members of the meddle class.

CERTAINLY NOT

Freshman: "Say, what's the idea of your wearing my raincoat?"

Roommate: "Well, you wouldn't want your new suit to get wet, would you?"

COME ON IN

Wise Guy (to incoming bus driver): "Well, Noah, is the ark full?"

Driver: "Nope, we need one more monkey; come on in."

NOT EASY

The head of a leading university says he is trying to develop a school the football team can be proud of.

AND YOU CAN'T PAY

Car sickness: The feeling you get every month when the payment falls due.

NO USE

"Are you ill?" asked the physician; "let me see your tongue."

"It's no use, Doctor," replied the patient; "no tongue can tell how bad I feel."

TWO PROBLEMS

A small boy was asked to write an essay in as few words as possible on two of life's greatest problems.

He wrote: "Twins."

PRETTY GOOD

Eastern visitor in a western village: "What a beautiful sunset!"

Native: "Yeah, not bad at all for a little place like this."

IT ISN'T FAIR

Typist: "But, Professor, isn't this the same exam you gave last year?"

Professor: "Yes, but I've changed the answers."

PUNS

A father once said to his son,
"The next time you make up a pun,
Go out in the yard
And kick yourself hard,
And I will begin when you've done."

CYNICISM

Cynic: One who thinks the world never changes, only short changes.

THAT EXPLAINS IT

Two small girls were playing together one afternoon in the park.

"I wonder what time it is," said one of them at last.

"Well, it can't be four o'clock yet," replied the other with magnificent logic, "because my mother said I was to be home at four, and I'm not."

IMPOSSIBLE

A guest of a small Southern hotel was awakened early one morning by a knock at his door. "What is it?" he called drowsily, without getting up.

"A telegram, boss," came a voice.

"Well, can't you push it under the door without waking me up?"

"No, suh; it's on a tray."

NEARSIGHTED GENTLEMAN

The clock on the station steeple had collected a coating of grime on its face and a steeple-jack had been commissioned to clean it. He mounted a tall ladder against the building to complete his chore when an inebriated gentleman passed by. He took one look at the man on the ladder, and then exclaimed: "Boy, is that guy nearsighted!"

NO MARKING

Every Thanksgiving the newspapers are full of diagrams showing how to carve a turkey. The trouble is that the birds we get never have dotted lines on them.

THAT HELPED

Ephraim, storekeeper in a small Vermont town, was greeted by a neighbor who consoled him on the loss of some of his merchandise during a fire.

"Did you lose much?" asked the friend.

"Not too much," came the laconic reply. "I'd just marked my stock down twenty per cent."

NOT MANY WILL KNOW

A Hollywood producer received a story entitled "The Optimist." He called his staff together and said: "Gentlemen, this title must be changed to something simpler. We're intelligent, and know what an optimist is, but how many of those morons who'll see the picture will know he's an eye doctor?"

GOOD REASON

Jack: "When I sat down to play the piano, they all laughed."

Tim: "Why?"

Jack: "There wasn't any piano stool."

LONG WAY FROM HOME

An Easterner was being driven by a rancher over a blistering and almost barren stretch of West Texas when a gaudy bird, new to him, scurried in front of them. The Easterner asked what it was.

"That's a Bird of Paradise," the rancher informed him.

The stranger rode on in silence for a while, then said:

"Pretty long way from home, isn't he?"

WRONG DIRECTION

The fog was dense and the boat had stopped when the old lady asked the Captain why he didn't go on.

"Can't see ahead, madam."

"But, Captain," she persisted, "I can see the stars overhead."

"Yes, ma'am," said the Captain, "but until the boilers bust we ain't goin' that way."

WE'VE SUFFERED, TOO

He had never had such a tough time in his life. First he got angina pectoris, followed by arteriosclerosis. Just as he was recovering from these he got pneumonia, and then pulmonary phthisis and tuberculosis. He had hardly survived these when he got appendicitis and pyorrhea. You wouldn't think he could do it, but he pulled through. It was the hardest spelling test he's ever had!

SEEMED REASONABLE

Mark Twain once asked a neighbor if he could borow a set of books which he was very anxious to use.

"You're welcome to read them in my library," answered the neighbor, "but it is my rule never to let my books leave my house."

Some weeks later the neighbor sent over to ask for the loan of Mark Twain's lawn mower.

"Certainly," replied Mark Twain, "but since I make it a rule never to let the lawn mower leave my lawn, you will be obliged to use it here."

THEY AGREE

The mother said firmly, "If you children don't agree, I shall have to take your pie away."

The younger replied, "But, Mother, we do agree; Bill wants the biggest piece, and so do I."

ADVICE

A young lawyer recently received the following letter from a tailor to whom he was indebted:

"Dear Sir: Kindly advise me by return mail when I may expect a remittance from you in settlement of my account."

"Yours truly,
"J. Snippen."

The lawyer immediately replied:

"Dear Sir: I have your request for advice and beg leave to say that not having received any retainer from you I cannot act. Upon receipt of your check for $250 I shall be very glad to look the matter up for you and acquaint you with the results of my investigations.

"Henry Jones"

IT AIN'T EASY

Some men smile in the evening, some men smile at dawn, but the man worth while is the man who can smile when his two front teeth are gone.　　*Iowa Green Gander*

CHAPTER IV

UNUSUAL FACTS AND ILLUSTRATIONS
NEW WORDS

If a contemporary Rip Van Winkle had slept for forty years and awakened today, he would have to go back to school before he could read a daily newspaper, according to Bergen Evans in *Think*. He would never have heard of atomic bombs or baby sitters, of coffee breaks or flying saucers, of eggheads, mambo or microfilm, of nylons, neptunium, or smog. And this is only the briefest sampling of the innumerable new words added to our language in a mere forty years. Since Shakespeare's time the number of words in the English language has increased from about 140,000 to somewhere between 700,000 and 800,000. Most of these new words have come, not from borrowing from other tongues, but from the adaptation of elements already in the language.

PERSISTENCE

The National Sales Executives Club has discovered a startling thing about salesmen.

48% of all salesmen make one call on a prospect and then stop calling.

20% make two calls — and quit.

7% make three calls — and quit.

5% make four calls — and quit.

20% make five or more calls — these close 80% of the total sales made.

A LOT EASIER

William Inge made a classic comment in his play The Dark at the Top of the Stairs: "Sometimes I wonder if it's not a lot easier to pioneer a country than it is to settle down in it."

EXCEPTIONAL

General Earle G. Wheeler, army chief of staff, addressing a graduating class, told about a father who faced a problem in filling out a college entrance application for a daughter. One question was, "What evidence of leadership does she show?" The father, a bit worried, wrote that "Louise shows no evidence of leadership, but she is a fine follower."

Right back came a letter from the dean of admissions saying: "We are pleased to accept Louise for admission. She will be the only follower in a class of 200 leaders."

EXERCISE

There is nothing, I think, more unfortunate than to have soft, chubby, fat-looking children who go to watch their school play basketball every Saturday and regard that as their week's exercise. *John F. Kennedy*

DANIEL WEBSTER

Abraham Lincoln told this story of Daniel Webster's boyhood:

Young Daniel was not noted for tidiness. One day in the district school the teacher told him if he appeared in school again with such dirty hands, she would thrash him. But the next day Daniel appeared with his hands in the same condition.

"Daniel," the teacher said in desperation, "hold out your hand!"

Daniel spat on his palm, rubbed it on the seat of his trousers, and held it out. The teacher surveyed it in disgust. "Daniel," she exclaimed, "if you can find me a hand in this school that is dirtier than this one here, I will let you off."

Daniel promptly held out his other hand. The teacher had to keep her word.

NO HAND BUT OURS

Shortly after the Second World War, a devastated city in England began its heartbreaking and wearying work of restoration. In the old city square had stood a large statue of Jesus Christ, with His hands outspread in an attitude of invitation. On the pedestal were carved the words, "Come unto me."

In the process of the restoration of the statue, with the aid of master artists and sculptors, the figure eventually was reassembled, except for the hands, of which no fragments could be discovered anywhere in the surrounding rubble. Someone made the suggestion that the artists, since the former hands could not be found, would have to fashion new hands.

Later came a public protest, couched in the words, "No, leave Him without hands!" So, today, in the public square of that English city, the restored statue of Christ stands without hands, and on its base are carved the words, "Christ has no hands but ours!"   *Sunshine Magazine*

DIVORCE

The oft-quoted figure of "one marriage in four" ending in divorce is misleading in that it relates current divorces to current marriages, whereas current divorces occur to marriages that took place at any time to still-living persons. A more adequate or sensitive measure is the divorce rate per 1,000 married females ages 15 years and over which has been under 10 (or 1%) each year since 1953. In terms of married couples, one in every 109 obtained a divorce in 1960.   *Survey Bulletin*

WHAT CAN YOU DO?

Weep, and you're called a baby; laugh, and you're called a fool; yield, and you're called a coward; stand, and you're a mule.

Smile, and they'll call you silly; frown, and they'll call you gruff. Put on a front like a millionaire, and somebody calls your bluff.

TWO SEAS

There are two seas in Palestine, both fed by the same river. One is brackish and dead; the other, sweet and living. What makes the difference? One receives and gives; the other receives and keeps.

HANDICAPS

Theodore Roosevelt started in life as a physical weakling, with no apparent qualities of leadership. Lincoln was laughed at as an ungainly country lawyer. Demosthenes stuttered.

NATURALLY

Official Washington has been chuckling over a story going the rounds concerning a man who was brought to the capital and put in charge of one of the many government agencies. A few days later one of his section chiefs asked permission to destroy a huge stack of useless documents.

"Very well," said the new department head officiously, "but be sure to make duplicate copies first."

HIS MOST IMPORTANT THOUGHT

When Daniel Webster was Secretary of State in President Fillmore's Cabinet, he gave a dinner one day at the Astor House to a few of his New York friends. There were about twenty at the table. Mr. Webster seemed wearied, and speaking but little, if at all, plunged into a sort of reverie, not calculated to enliven his friends.

One of Webster's friends endeavored to get him into conversation. He spoke to Mr. Webster, but the Secretary of State merely raised his head and answered simply, then crept back into his cave.

Once more the man said to Webster, "Mr. Secretary, what was the most important thought that ever occupied your mind." Here was a thumper for Webster, and so thought everyone at the table.

Mr. Webster slowly passed his hand over his forehead, and in a low voice said to his friend near him, "Is there anyone here who does not know me?"

"No, sir, they all know you, and all are your friends."

Then Webster looked up over the table, and said in clear, resonant tones, "The most important thought that ever occupied my mind was that of my individual responsibility to God."

LAST WORDS

This is the last of earth! I am content.
John Quincy Adams

See in what peace a Christian can die.
Joseph Addison

Let me die in my old uniform. God forgive me for ever putting on any other.

> *Benedict Arnold* (calling for his old Continental uniform of a major general)

I have fought a good fight, I have finished my course, I have kept the faith; henceforth there is laid up for me a crown, which God, the righteous Judge, will give me at that day. ... That is my testimony — write it down — that is my testimony.

> *Lyman Beecher* (Presbyterian clergyman; quoting the words of St. Paul)

But I have to. So little done. So much to do.

> *Alexander Graham Bell* (dictating, though his wife said "Please don't hurry")

Take me home. I must go home.

> *Phillips Brooks* (Episcopal bishop)

O Lord God Almighty, as Thou wilt!

> *James Buchanan*

Weep not for me but yourselves: I go to the Father of our Lord Jesus Christ, who will, no doubt, through the mediation of his Blessed Son, receive me, though a sinner, where I hope that we ere long shall meet to sing the new song and remain for everlastingly happy, world without end.   *John Bunyan* (author of Pilgrim's Progress)

With the best that was in me I have tried to write more happiness into the world.

> *Frances Hodgson Burnett* (author)

I have tried so hard to do right.   *Grover Cleveland*

Into Thy hands, O Lord, I commend my spirit.

> *Christopher Columbus*

I were miserable if I might not die. ... Thy Kingdom come, Thy Will be done.   *John Donne*

Tell me, Alexander, on your soul and conscience, do you believe that anything of mine will live?

> *Alexandre Dumas*

Why fear death? It is the most beautiful adventure of life. ... Why fear death?

> *Charles Frohman* (theatrical manager)

God bless our American institutions. May they grow better day by day.   *Samuel Gompers* (labor leader)

Oh, do not cry. Be good children, and we shall all meet in Heaven.
Andrew Jackson

I am at peace with all the world, but there is still a lot of work I could do. I don't know how the people will feel toward me, but I shall take to the grave my love for them which has sustained me through life.
Robert M. La Follette

In your passage through this life remember the sufferings of Jesus Christ.
Michelangelo

I have a terrific headache! *Franklin D. Roosevelt*

Well, Martha! . . . Glad to see you looking so well.
Senator Robert A. Taft (to his wife)

I'll never give up trust in Jesus. How could I let that go?
Cornelius Vanderbilt

'Tis well.
George Washington

ATHEISM

Only in Atheism does the spring rise higher than the source, the effect exist without the cause, life come from a stone, blood from a turnip, a silk purse from a sow's ear, a Beethoven Symphony or a Bach Fugue from a kitten's walking across the keys.

James M. Gillis, in Chicago Sunday Tribune Magazine of Books.

NOT QUITE

A Hungarian farmer, professing to be a whole-hearted Communist, was asked why he was an atheist. He replied, "Karl Marx was an atheist, Lenin was an atheist, Stalin is an atheist, and I am an atheist — thank God."
Presbyterian Life

LONG TIME AGO

In an elevator the other day, we overheard one sweet thing say to another: "But, my dear, don't be so utterly pre-atomic!"
The Montrealer

THE HEAVENS

On a beautiful starlit night Einstein was strolling the Princeton Promenade. He looked up at the sky and said, with a weary sigh, "Anyway, THAT the atom cannot destroy!"
Hollywood Reporter

THE BIBLE

Tennyson makes over four hundred allusions to passages in the Bible. In Browning over six hundred Biblical allusions are found. In Shakespeare there are seven hundred cases of such references. In Milton they run up into many thousands. It is not a question of dogma, or theology, or religion: knowledge of the Bible is a requirement of general intelligence.

Robert Stuart MacArthur, Wesleyan Christian Advocate

HIS BROTHER

A boy was carrying a younger brother up a steep hill. A stranger asked, "Isn't that a heavy burden?" The lad replied, "This isn't a burden. This is my brother."

If, first of all, we are our brother's brother, it will be much easier to be our brother's keeper.

The Upper Room

THEY COME OUT RIGHT

Some little girls were told the story of Abraham and his sacrifice of Isaac. The teacher, with a dramatic touch, made it live. Suddenly, as the story approached its climax, a nervous little girl burst out: "Oh, please don't go on — this story is too terrible." But a second little girl spoke up at once: "Oh, Mary, don't be so silly. This is one of God's stories and they always come out right."

Gerald Kennedy, Pulpit Preaching

CHRISTMAS

I have always thought of Christmas time when it has come round, as a good time; a kind, forgiving, charitable time; the only time I know, in the long calendar of the year, when men and women seem by one consent to open their shut-up hearts freely, and to think of people below them as if they really were fellow passengers to the grave, and not another race of creatures bound on other journeys.

Charles Dickens

A LASTING GIFT

A friend described a present that was always in his stocking each Christmas morn of his childhood: "It was a candy potato, like an all-day sucker. I would lick only a little of it on Christmas Day. Then I would put it away. Whenever my spirits were low, I would lick it a little. Sometimes I could make it last as long as August."

If only we could make all the Christmas sweetness last until August! *KVP Philosopher*

A WISH

A four-year old attended prayer meeting not long ago with his parents. When he knelt to say his prayers before going to bed upon his return, he prayed: "Dear Lord, we had a good time at church tonight. I wish you could have been there." *Christian Advocate*

CIVILIZATION

A tall cowhand wearing a ten gallon hat was sauntering around in a large department store and the salesgirl asked if she might help him. He replied:

"No, ma'am, I reckon not. I ain't never seen so much I could do without." *Northwestern Bell*

TOO LATE

He always said he would retire when he had made a million clear. And so he toiled into the night from day to day, from year to year. At last he put his ledgers up, and laid his stock aside; but when he started out to live, he found he'd already died.

IS IT THAT BAD?

This world is full of fools; and not to see one pass, you must shut yourself up alone, and break your looking-glass.

ACTION

A teacher told her class to write a four-line verse that showed action. One boy wrote:

"A boy walked down a railroad track,
A train was coming fast;
The boy jumped off the railroad track
To let the train go past."

The teacher said the verse did not show enough action, so the boy revised it as follows:

"A boy walked down a railroad track,
A train was coming fast;
The train jumped off the railroad track
To let the boy go past."

NO TIME TO ARGUE

The man who once most wisely said, "Be sure you're right, then go ahead," might well have added this, to wit: "When you know you're wrong, be sure to quit."

SPEAKING ILL

The form of criticism which has far too many votaries for the happiness of mankind is backbiting. One of the most deplorable weaknesses of human nature is the love of tittle-tattle — cutting throats behind backs. Does any good come of backbiting? Noble are the men and women who refuse to lend themselves to this practice. Theirs is the gospel of not saying ill if they cannot say good.

The Uplift

TIME

When time who steals our years away
Shall steal our pleasures too,
The mem'ry of the past will stay
And half our joys renew.   *Moore*

'Tis God gives skill,
But not without men's hands:
He could not make
Antonio Stradivari's violins
Without Antonio

George Eliot

EXAMS

Why worry over exams? You have two alternatives —
your teacher is either easy or hard. If he is easy, you have
nothing to worry about. If he is hard, you have two alternatives — either you study hard or you bluff. If you study
hard, you don't have to worry. If you bluff, you have two
alternatives — either your bluff works or it doesn't. If it
works, you have nothing to worry about. If it doesn't you
have two alternatives — either you are conditioned, or you
flunk. If you are conditioned, you needn't worry. If you
flunk, you won't have to worry any longer. Why worry?

OR AN ARGUMENT

A perplexed motorist thinks that an arm protruding from
the car ahead means the driver is —

1. Knocking ashes off his cigar.
2. Going to turn to the left.
3. Telling a small boy to shut up — he doesn't want
   any red pop.
4. Going to turn to the right.
5. Pointing out a scenic spot.
6. Going to back up.
7. Feeling for rain.
8. Telling friend wife, "I'm sure the kitchen door is
   locked."
9. Saluting a passing motorist.
10. Going to stop.

YOU CAN FOOL THEM

Select any number you wish, then double it. To the total
add 10. Divide by 2, and from that resulting number sub-
tract the number which you originally selected. The answer
will be 5. The key to this little puzzler is that the answer
will always be just one-half of the number which you tell
your friend to add.

IT'S JUST LIKE THIS

Any ordinary sentence can be made to have as many
meanings as it can have variations of inflection. Let us give

an example: If we were to say, "I never said he stole money," what would it mean? It's all in the way we say it. There are six words in that sentence; by emphasizing each word separately, we get six different meanings. Read them aloud and see:

I never said he stole money.
I *never* said he stole money.
I never *said* he stole money.
I never said *he* stole money.
I never said he *stole* money.
I never said he stole *money.*

ROAD HAZARDS

The road is strewn with motor cars, and folks would like to know why dangers stare us in the face where'er we chance to go. Investigations come galore, committees probe the cause; men check the car, its bolts and brakes, and scan the motor laws.

They search the reasons, buried deep, but in the end reveal that accidents are mostly caused by the nut that holds the wheel.

"NOTUSE"

The following notice was actually posted on the bulletin board of one of the mountain towns:

NOTUSE

Los'em self one caff. Red all over. One foot white. Other three same like. Bin loss 3 daze. Yesterday, today, tomorrow. Ane one finer, give everybody five bucks.

BONER

Here are a few educational "boners" that English children made in recent tests, and which have just been published in London. The effect of American made "movies" is very evident as the very first "boner" illustrates.

A lad asked to identify the jungle Tarzan gave this definition: "Tarzan is a short name for the American flag. The full name is Tarzan Stripes."

Other "boners" made by the 11-year-olds were:

A crisis is a thing which hangs up in the winter and comes down in the summer a butterfly.

Matrimony is a place where souls suffer for a time because of their sin.

A republic is a country where no one can do anything in private.

Bookkeeping is the art of not returning books borrowed.

Contralto is a low sort of music that only ladies can sing.

The spine is a bundle of bones which runs up and down the back and holds the ribs together.

HOW MUCH IS A BILLION?

You often hear reports of government spending that mention the word "billion." Do you know how much a "billion dollars" actually is? Well, someone has done some figuring, and puts a billion dollars in terms we can all understand:

If each soldier carried a 50 pound pack of dollar bills, it would take 42,500 men to carry a billion dollars;

Or, if each truck carried 5 tons of dollar bills, it would take 212 trucks to hold a billion dollars;

Or, if you laid dollar bills end to end, they would circle the earth 4 times;

Or, if you covered a sidewalk 8-½ feet wide with dollar bills, it would make a sidewalk 2,442 miles long, or from Washington, D. C. to San Francisco, California.

TROUBLES

He wrecked his car, he lost his job, and yet throughout his life he took his troubles like a man — he blamed them on his wife.

UNUSED OPPORTUNITIES

I tore the first leaf from my calendar, and dropped it into the wastebasket. The first chapter of my New Year, with all its possibilities, was closed.

No aroma of used opportunities arose from that torn

leaf — it fluttered from my fingers and fell — just a useless scrap of paper. And yet thirty days ago it was alive and vibrant with possibilities. There were days in it when I might have cheered the sorrowful, days when I might have spoken the encouraging word, days when I might have visited the sick, days when I might have lifted the burden of those oppressed.

But today, the bit of paper is crumpled and soiled and torn, and the chapter is closed.

I reflect. Must my whole year be a record of unused opportunities? And at the end, will my record flutter into nothingness, and lie forgotten and crumpled like the torn piece of paper?

Beulah G. Squires in The Christian

CHAPTER V

STORIES OF PERSONS AND EVENTS

TEEN AGE ENGLISH

Representative J. Vaughan Gary of Virginia discovered that teen-age talk isn't reserved for teen-age communication. He received a polite letter from a high school girl requesting material she needed for a classroom report.

"She concluded her courteous letter with, 'Thank you and all that jazz,'" Representative Gary said.

Nathaniel Benchley, son of Robert, the late, great humorist, told this story about his father: He was about to leave a club in Hollywood. He asked a man in uniform to summon a cab.

"Sir," the man replied, "you are addressing a rear admiral in the United States navy."

"Very well," said Benchley, "then get me a battleship."

TO MAKE GOOD-MEN

Russell Lynes begins the concluding chapter in his book, *A Surfeit of Honey*, with a number of rather significant observations. He reminds us that there are sixty-seven million Americans who have jobs today — more than ever before. The national personal income is over 300 billion. Tiffany and Company, recently advertised a diamond necklace of "simple elegance" for $168,300, including tax!

The manufacturers of the Continental car which sells for $10,000, urge their customers to "feel the thrill of being conservative."

These are indicative of a state of mind. They reflect a pattern of values that is having its effect upon higher education. Current among large segments of our population is the idea that the chief purpose of an education is to enable a young man or a young woman to enjoy these good times — to buy that necklace or own that car! There is an old maxim about the object of an education being to make good men. Dean Charles Osgood of Princeton suggests that this maxim has undergone a strange atrophy. Today it reads: The object of an education is to make good — period."   *Robert D. Swanson*

THE BEST PLACE ON EARTH

One evening when Thomas Edison came home from work, his wife said to him, "You've worked long enough without a rest. You must go on a vacation."

"But where on earth would I go?" asked Mr. Edison.

"Just decide where you would rather be than anywhere else on earth," suggested the wife.

Mr. Edison hesitated. "Very well," he said finally, "I'll go tomorrow."

The next morning he was back at work in his laboratory.

WHO OUGHT TO BE BOSS?

The question "Who ought to be boss?" is like asking, "Who ought to be tenor in the quartet?" Obviously, the man who can do the job.   *Henry Ford*

HE HANDLED HECKLERS

Benjamin Franklin, with his sagacity and wit, was a man who thoroughly enjoyed trimming hecklers down to size. During the early days of the American Republic, he spoke many times on that great document, the Constitution of the United States.

After one such stirring speech an uncouth fellow rose and boldly walked a few paces toward the platform. "Aw, them words don't mean nothin' a-tall!" he shouted at Franklin. "Where's all that happiness you say it guarantees us?"

Franklin smiled benevolently at the questioner, and quickly, blandly, Old Ben replied, "My friend, the Constitution only guarantees the American people the right to pursue happiness. You have to catch it yourself!"

Sunshine Magazine

WASHINGTON, D. C.

Senator Carl Curtis (R., Neb.) described Washington as the place where every politician over 35 thinks he ought to be President and every politician under 35 is sure he's going to be President.

RESOLVED

Resolved, to live with all my might while I do live. Resolved, never to lose one moment of time, to improve it in the most profitable way I can. Resolved, never to do anything which I should despise or think meanly in another. Resolved, never to do anything out of revenge. Resolved, never to do anything which I should be afraid to do if it were the last hour of my life.

Jonathan Edwards, American theologian and preacher (1703-58).

THE HISTORY OF LIBERTY

The history of liberty is a history of the limitation of governmental power, not the increase of it. When we resist, therefore, the concentration of power, we are resisting the processes of death, because concentration of power is what always precedes the destruction of human liberties. *Woodrow Wilson*

A FANATIC

Mr. Dooley, the American humorist, once defined a fanatic as "a man who does what he thinks th' Lord wud do if He only knew th' facts in the case."

REDUCING

Senator Karl Mundt tells of an overweight senator who consulted his doctor on reducing.

"Can you get rid of the fat where I have it the most?" the senator asked.

"Certainly, but you'd look pretty silly running around without your head."

TIME TO PAY

In the 1920s, when Owen D. Young was wrestling with war debts and encountering resentment from the French, he reported that Uncle Sam was painted as a Shylock in some sections of the press. Young used to tell an imaginary story of General John J. Pershing returning to the tomb of Lafayette and, with his hand raised in salute, declaring:

"Lafayette, we are here. And this time we want our money."

TAKING NO CHANCE

Representative Earl Wilson was perplexed on a train trip to Scotland by an aging Scot who got off at each stop, raced to the station, and then raced back to the train. He barely made his coach at each station. Unable to contain his curiosity Wilson asked him what he found so important at each station.

"Well," said the Scot, "you see my doctor has told me I have a bad heart that might go any minute, so I'm buying my trip station to station."

ONE KIND OF SACRIFICE

The novelist George Eliot says of her character, Tito, "He was to be depended on to make any sacrifice that was not unpleasant." Such easy so-called sacrifices cost nothing. But seriously to keep service for all sort of folks at the center of one's purpose involves readiness to deny ourselves.   *Halford E. Luccock*

A BALANCED LIFE

Charles Evans Hughes, who was Chief Justice of the Supreme Court and a great Christian, once gave this picture of what he called "a balanced life." He said it had faith without credulity, courage without pugnacity, meekness with power, self respect without vanity.
                    Halford E. Luccock

SO LIVE

Helen Keller, the wonderful girl who became deaf and dumb and blind as a young child, and grew up into one of the most marvelous women of the world, wrote a word to all persons who have sight. She wrote, "Live as though you were going blind tomorrow." She pleaded with all to look at God's world — really look at it! Jesus said, "Consider the lilies . . ." Consider them! Look at and consider all the beauties of our Father's world. If we see beauty and give thanks, that's real worship.

Halford E. Luccock

HOW DO YOU ANSWER?

Chief Justice Marshall, of the United States Supreme Court, used to narrate the following correspondence on a point of honor between Governor Giles of Virginia and the famous Patrick Henry:

"Sir," wrote the governor, "I understand that you have called me a bobtail politician. I wish to know if it be true, and if true, your meaning. W. G. Giles."

Patrick Henry's reply was:

"Sir, I do not recollect calling you a bobtail politician at any time, but think it probable that I have. I can't say what I did mean; but if you will tell me what you think I meant, I will say whether you are correct or not. Very respectfully, Patrick Henry."

SORRY

Abraham Lincoln was noted for his pungent and appropriate wit. He was resting with his campaign manager in a hotel lobby. As usual the village cut-ups congregated there, and one, bolder than the rest, remarked, "Mr. Lincoln, your speech was good, but there were some points in it that are quite beyond my reach."

The simple Lincoln looked up and chuckled: "Then I am sorry for you. I once had a dog that had the same trouble with fleas." *Association Men*

DON'T BLAME HIM

Mark Twain spent one summer at Riverside, N. Y. A suburban fish peddler, with a raucous voice and a tin horn, passed the house frequently. Finally, one morning, Mark said:

"That fellow has been here twice every day this week. Such persistency ought to be rewarded. I'm going to buy a fish of him," which he accordingly did. Prepared for luncheon, the fish was found to be highly unsatisfactory, and when the peddler appeared in the afternoon, the humorist went out and hailed him.

"See here!" said Mark, with warmth, "that fish wasn't eatable. It was too old."

"Well, it wasn't my fault, Boss," replied the man indignantly. "I give you two chances every day this week to buy that fish, and if you was foolish enough to wait till it was spoiled, don't blame me."

A TRUE STORY?

Once upon a time, they say, a man invented a mousetrap. He believed his fortune would be made by its sale if he could get President Lincoln to recommend it. After a long, persistent effort, he secured an audience with the President and received the following recommendation, which will apply to many things besides mousetraps:

"For the sort of people who want this sort of thing, this is the sort of thing that sort of people will want."

LANCELOT

The late Channing Pollock, the playwright, told of his friend "Fred," a linen salesman. Fred had never earned more than forty dollars a week in all his life, and on that salary he and Clara had bought a little home in New Jersey. Their two boys had been sent through college.

"When I last saw Fred," said Mr. Pollock, "he was shabbily dressed. I asked him why he couldn't treat himself a little better, now that the house was paid for, and the boys were doing well.

" 'I carry a lot of life insurance,' Fred answered; 'I've got to be awfully sure that Clara's all right when I'm gone.' He turned away rather shamefacedly. A stray sunbeam fell across his shoulders, and suddenly I saw, not a shiny suit of clothes, but a shining armor. Not Fifth Avenue, but Camelot, and a plumed knight, with a sword at his side, and his lady's colors worn across his coat of mail.

" 'What's the difference,' I thought, 'between that man and Lancelot?' There are millions of Freds — all around us. Certain sophisticated youngsters are telling us that sentiment is bunk; that loyalty and nobility and idealism and self-sacrifice are applesauce. Sentiment and nobility and love are immortal."

PERFECTION

An Italian duke came upon a workman who seemed to be taking infinite care and pains in his work. He asked the laborer, "For what will the box you are making be used?"

"Flowers will be planted in it, sir."

Amused, the Duke continued, "It will be filled with dirt. Why take such pains to make each joint and surface perfect?"

"I love perfect things," the man replied.

"Ah, wasted effort! No one will observe its perfection. A mere flower box does not require such perfection."

"But my spirit does," insisted the man. "Do you suppose that the Carpenter of Nazareth ever made anything less perfect than He could? . . ."

Angrily, the duke replied, "Sacrilege! Your impudence deserves a flogging. What is your name?"

The reply came: "Michaelangelo, sir."

Rev. A. Purnell Bailey

FOR OTHER MEN

Strange is our situation here upon earth. Each of us comes for a short visit, not knowing why, yet seeming to divine a purpose: There is one thing we do know: man is here for the sake of other men — above all, for those upon whose well-being our own happiness depends . . . and for the countless unknown souls with whose fate we are connected by a bond of sympathy. Many times a day do I realize how much my own outer and inner life is built upon the labors of my fellowmen, both living and dead, and how earnestly I must exert myself in order to give in return as much as I have received. My peace of mind is often troubled by the depressing sense that I have borrowed too heavily from the work of other men. *Albert Einstein*

POVERTY

A young musician complained to Brahms of his poverty which made it a problem even to buy manuscript paper. Brahms silently went to his cabinet and extracted the original draft of his Requiem. "Look at this manuscript," he said. "You will see that the manuscript paper is of different brands and shapes. I could not afford to buy a lot of paper all at once." *Nicholas Slonimsky, Etude*

REST

It is reported that when Diogenes was told he should take a rest, since he was an old man, he replied, "If I were running in the stadium, ought I to slacken my pace when approaching the goal. Ought I not rather put on speed?" . . . Good sense will dictate when we need to change our load and vary our pace, but we must keep on going, somehow — to the end. That's part of the armament required to combat the perils of age.

Everett W. Palmer, The Pastor

ACHIEVEMENT

At about the age when many men begin to consider themselves crossing over to the shady side of life — the half-century mark — Sir Christopher Wren, who built magnificent St. Paul's Cathedral in London in the seventeenth century, was entering enthusiastically upon a new career in a new profession. After serving as professor of astronomy at Gresham College and Oxford, he turned architect.

In the forty-one years after his forty-eighth birthday this amazing man executed fifty-three churches and cathedrals, most of which still stand as monuments to his greatness. Like the man James Whitcomb Riley wrote of who had "lived to three-score and ten and had the hang of it now and could do it again," Sir Christopher discovered the secret of living a second life and doing another life's work.

Robert R. Updegraff

WHAT HE SEES

Lawrence of Arabia told a friend the story of a conversation he once had with an Arab companion, as they rode camels by night across the desert. The brilliant stars prompted him to inform his untutored companion of the discoveries of modern astronomy. The Arab listened with attention until Lawrence was through. Then he replied in simple confidence: "Yes, it is true. The foreigner looks through his wonder-glasses and beholds millions of stars. And that is all. He is proud of his knowledge. But the Arab looks up and sees only a few stars. But behind the stars he sees God."

Rev. Robert W. Etter, Religious Telescope

HARDSHIP

If you have the idea that physical perfection is necessary to success in your chosen field, take a look at this even dozen of famous men and the handicaps that failed to slow them; Lord Byron had a clubfoot; Robert Louis Stevenson and John Keats had tuberculosis. Charles Steinmetz and Alexander Pope were hunchbacks; Admiral Nelson had only one eye; Edgar Allan Poe was a psychoneurotic; Charles Darwin was an invalid; Julius Caesar was an epileptic; Thomas Edison and Ludwig von Beethoven were deaf, and Peter Stuyvesant had a wooden leg. *Wilfred Funk*

INFALLIBLE

On one occasion when Henry Ward Beecher was in the midst of an eloquent speech, some wag in the audience crowed like a cock. It was done to perfection and the audience was in a gale of helpless laughter.

But Mr. Beecher stood perfectly calm. He stopped speaking, listened till the crowing ceased. While the audience was still laughing he pulled out his watch. Then he said, slowly:

"That's strange. My watch says it is only ten o'clock. But there can't be any mistake about it. It must be morning, for the instincts of the lower animals are absolutely infallible."

DON'T WORRY

Winston Churchill once had to take to dinner a young lady who had decided political views which were in opposition to his views. Mr Churchill had just grown what he considered a very handsome moustache, the appearance of which seemed to incense the young lady.

"Mr. Churchill," said the young lady, "I care for neither your politics nor your moustache."

"Don't distress yourself, my dear young lady," returned Mr. Churchill; "you are not likely to come in contact with either."

ENOUGH

Milton was one day asked by a friend whether he would instruct his daughters in the different languages.

"No, sir," he said; "one tongue is sufficient for any woman."

SILENT MEN

Some men of history won fame because they didn't talk much. They said little and did much. These men were not morose or unsocial. They were simply not loquacious.

George Washington was one of the silent men of our American scene. He talked when it was necessary, was not hesitant when directions were to be given or advice sought, but the famed Virginian was not given to small talk, nor noted as a conversationalist.

Lincoln had his silent hours when he appeared to be withdrawn from the social chatter about him, and was not of the mind to relate incidents of old Indiana and Illinois days. He had his brooding periods, which on occasion were shrouded in deep melancholy.

Calvin Coolidge had a reputation as a silent president, sparing of speech and loving laconic expressions. But when he was in the mood of a mind to talk, the Vermonter did not lack for words. *Sunshine Magazine*

ELEVEN POOR BOYS

John Adams, second President of the United States, was the son of a grocer of very moderate means. The only start he had was a good education.

Andrew Jackson was born in a log hut in North Carolina, and was reared in the beautiful pine woods for which the state is famous.

James K. Polk spent the earlier years of his life helping to dig a living out of a new farm in North Carolina. He was afterward a clerk in a country store.

Millard Fillmore was the son of a New York farmer, and his home was a humble one. He learned the business of a clothier.

James Buchanan was born in a small town in the Allegheny Mountains. His father cut the logs and built the house in what was then a wilderness.

Abraham Lincoln was the son of a wretchedly poor farmer in Kentucky, and lived in a log cabin until he was twenty-one years old.

Andrew Johnson was aprenticed to a tailor at the age of ten years by his widowed mother. He was never able to attend school, and picked up all the education he ever had.

Ulysses S. Grant lived the life of a village boy, in a plain house on the banks of the Ohio River, until he was seventeen years of age.

James A. Garfield was born in a log cabin. He worked on the farm until he was strong enough to use carpenter's tools, when he learned the trade. He afterwards worked on a canal.

Grover Cleveland's father was a Presbyterian minister with a small salary and a large family. The boys had to earn their living.

William McKinley's early home was plain and comfortable, and his father was able to keep him at school.

Rocky Mountain Advocate

ART

The story is told of the famous artist, Holman Hunt, that when he informed his friends that he was planning to paint a picture of Christ they said it was impossible. The true artist, they insisted, can paint only what he can see. "But I am going to see Him," Hunt is said to have replied. "I will work by His side in the carpenter shop. I will walk with Him over the hills of Galilee. I will go with Him among the poor, the blind, the naked, the lepers. I will

travel with Him to Calvary and climb the cross with Him, until I see Him and know Him, and then I will paint Him."
William T. McElroy, Christian Observer

GOOD EMPLOYEES

When people are achieving some measure of their potential and are happy people, they are good employees, and they are making the company and the 'boss' look good, too.
E. J. Thomas, Business Management

TOO LATE AND TOO EARLY

Somerset Maugham, the writer, recuperating in London from a recent bout with the flu, was telephoned by a lady admirer. She wondered if she might send fruit and flowers.

Replied the 88-year-old Maugham: "It's too late for fruit — too early for flowers."

BE CAREFUL

As the House was working its way through the civil rights bill, drafted by lawyers, many nonlawyer members complained they could not understand the legalistic language. Representative George Grant recalled a case where the defendant inquired if he could ask the prosecutor a question.

"Are you a lawyer?" asked the prosecutor.

"No, but if I had known how little it takes to be one, I would have been one," replied the witness.

JOHN WESLEY

During World War II a young friend of this writer wrote back a letter from London. He had just been out that day to visit the old home of John Wesley. He described it very beautifully in the letter: "When I walked into John Wesley's prayer room it was like walking back through the pages of history. It seemed to me that John Wesley was still alive, that he was around some place, likely to step in at any moment. There beside the window was his old chair where he loved to sit and study. There on the rug was a bare spot that suggested the imprint of knees. On the table was lying his old Bible as though it had just been laid down a few moments before. There was an aroma of God in that room that 200 years could not erase. I think I'm a better person because I visited there."

Rev. Thurston Masters, Arkansas Methodist

AMERICAN

Senator Kenneth B. Keating commenting wistfully on a letter from a housewife-constituent who asked for higher tariffs, mused:

"So far as I can make out, a typical American is one who comes home from an Italian movie in his German car, has Brazilian coffee out of an English mug, sits down in his Danish chair, and picks up a Japanese ballpoint pen to write to his congressman to support 'buy American' legislation."

THRIFT

A favorite story of Nelson Rockefeller is about his famous grandfather, John D. Rockefeller. A young employee entered his grandfather's office to find the millionaire on his hands and knees looking for a dropped dime.

"You don't need that dime, Mr. Rockefeller," said the employee.

"Young man," he admonished, "don't you know a dime represents 5 per cent interest on $2 for an entire year?"

NEW IDEAS

A man who had poor health worked in a print shop. He found that it helped him in his work to stand on a rubber mat. The shock of the machinery was lessened, and he had more strength for his work.

Other workers in the shop noticed the mat, thought it was a fine idea, and whenever he would leave the machine, they would come and borrow the mat. The printer would come back and find the mat gone. Displeased with this arrangement, the printer thought to improve the rubber mat idea. He cut pieces of rubber into little squares and nailed them on the soles of his shoes. In this way he carried his mat with him wherever he went.

It worked so well that the other men in the shop came and asked him to make rubber mats for their shoes. Before long, the "rubber mat man" was busy every noon cutting out rubber heels for his shop mates.

The man's name was O'Sullivan.

Those rubber heels have been made by the hundreds of thousands, and sold all over the world. The business was born when O'Sullivan let an idea come into his head. The little idea developed into a great industry that has made life easier for thousands of men and women.

That wasn't the last idea in the world. For every old idea there are a thousand new ones, undiscovered and untried. Next to character, ideas are the most valuable things. And it doesn't take any money to get one.

IT WILL CONTINUE TO BE

Without God there could be no American form of government, nor an American way of life. Recognition of the Supreme Being is the first — the most basic — expression of Americanism. Thus the founding fathers of America saw it, and thus, with God's help, it will continue to be.

Dwight D. Eisenhower

TWO REASONS

The late columnist Arthur Brisbane declined to accept William Randolph Hearst's offer of a six months' paid vacation in appreciation for his good work.

"There are two reasons why I will not accept your generous offer, Mr. Hearst," said Brisbane. "The first is that if I quit writing my column for half a year, it might affect the circulation of your newspapers. The second reason is that it might not!"

CHAPTER VI

HELPFUL SELECTIONS FROM SPEECHES AND OTHER SOURCES

IT ISN'T FREE

There is no such thing as a free lunch — not even when the Government provides it.

Every lunch has to be paid for — by somebody.

The same is true of Government aids, benefits, and services.

They are not free.

All of these things have to be paid for by somebody, and that somebody is "we, the people."

There is no such thing as "federal funds." That term is a wolf dressed up in sheep's clothing, and it deceives a lot of us into feeling what we get from the Government is free.

Congress does not possess an Aladdin's Lamp, nor a financial wishing well.

Neither does the Administration in Washington.

Every dollar the Congress appropriates, and every dollar the Government spends, comes out of the earnings of the people.

There is no one else to pay the bills.

The more the Government spends for free school lunches, for free inland waterways, for free terminal and airway services, for free hospital and medical services, for free farm price support programs, the more the Government must tax us.

And that means that each of us has less to spend, or to save.

W. G. Vollmer, President of Texas & Pacific Railway.

YOUR FAULTS

Think of your own faults the first part of the night when

you are awake, and of the faults of others the latter part of the night when you are asleep.

Chinese Proverb

MORE LIKE A TREE

I would like to become more like a tree. May I yet grow in very virtue that God has given me, bear fruit on my branches, and, moreover, secure my soul in sturdy roots, that it may direct and strengthen me in daily living.

Ludwig von Beethoven

A PRAYER

For a College Student

I pray Thy special care for a student, far away from home, in college, where his life is an adventure among new friends and his studies an adventure in new fields of knowledge. As he tests for himself the standards he has learned at home, may he find that they apply to new situations. May he have an open, eager mind, making good use of his opportunities to broaden his background of understanding as he prepares for the work he will choose. During his busy days, even though he gives little thought to his family, may the knowledge of their loving confidence be as heart-warming as the glowing coals of a hearth. I thank Thee that he has the privilege of these student years. May he learn well, give as well as receive, and graduate ready to work and serve creatively. Amen.

First Presbyterian Church of Evanston, Illinois, Bulletin

IN OLDEN TIMES

One of these days a child is going to come home from school and say to you: "Grandpa, we read something in the history book today, and I want you to tell me if it is true — really true. It said in the history book that in the olden times," — that is right now, of course — "that in the olden times our ancestors used to put up our houses one brick at a time. Tell me grandpa, is that really true?"

Well, you will have no alternative but to reply: "Well, yes, that is right."

The little child will say, "Grandpa, the Sumerians put up their houses one brick at a time 4,000 years before you, and you mean you hadn't learned a better way in 4,000 years?"

You will have to say, "Yes, that is right."

They will come home the next day and say, "Grandpa, we read something in the history book today. I want to know if it is true that in the olden times people used to send written messages in this way to one and another. They would write it down on a piece of paper, carry it out, and put it in a red, white, and blue box on the corner. It would lie there for several hours and a man would come around in a vehicle and pick it up, and then it would be transmitted to another city, taken out to the residential district, and then a man in a gray uniform would trudge around from house to house delivering these messages. Grandpa, is that really true?"

We have to give the same answer. "That is right."

Well, the child will say, "Do you mean they didn't have 'Instafac,' — instantaneous facsimile transmission?" In that day a person will put a message in the machine, dial the number of the recipient, push the button, and instantaneously the message will be reproduced at the other end.

Well, in this respect as in others, I think they will forgive us for a reason that will seem eminently sensible to them, because (as they will see it) we were a primitive people who did not have the advantages of modern science.

J. Philip Wernette, Professor, University of Michigan

MAKE ME AN INSTRUMENT

Lord,
Make me an instrument of Thy peace.
Where there is hatred,
Let me sow love;
Where there is injury, pardon;
Where there is doubt, faith;
Where there is despair, hope;
Where there is darkness, light;
Where there is sadness, joy.

O Divine Master,
Grant that I may seek
Not so much to be consoled,
As to console;
To be understood, as to understand.
To be loved, as to love;
For it is in giving
That we receive;
It is in pardoning
That we are pardoned;
It is in dying
That we are born to eternal life.

Francis of Assissi

COOPERATION

We hear about the skillful man,
The man who leads the line,
But seldom do we hear about
The other ninety-nine;
The men who bravely battle in
A world of enterprise,
Who form the steppingstones on which
The skillful man may rise.

The wheel of life is not cast
That issues from the mould;
On each small part depends the heart
Which hath the greater hold;
The outer pinions may revolve
And glisten in the sun,
But it's the oil-stained cogs beneath
On which those pinions run.

Cooperation is the word
That's worthy of a thought;
By that alone can all men gain
The brotherhood long sought;
Each man has got his part to play,
Each man can hope to shine,
But he who leads, most surely needs
The other ninety-nine.

THOUGHTS

Greater opportunities are the rewards of past accomplishments.

Knowledge humbleth the great man, astonishes the common man, and puffeth up the little man.

A man who has committed a mistake and doesn't correct it, is making another mistake.

REMEMBER

It may be that there will be a lot of people in Heaven just as surprised to see you as you will be surprised to see them.

IN BUSINESS

When a certain young man grew tired of working for others, he went into business for himself. Later a friend asked him how it was to be his own boss.

"I don't know," he replied. "The police won't let me park in front of my own place of business; tax collectors tell me how to keep my books; my bankers tells me how much balance I must maintain; freight agents tell me how my goods must be packed and addressed; customers tell me how my goods must be made; federal, state, county, and local agencies tell me how to keep records; the union tells me who I can work, and how, and when; and, on top of all that, I just went broke!"

LOOKING AHEAD

What do we want of this vast, worthless area, this region of savages and wild beasts, of shifting sands and whirlpools of dust, of cactus and prairie dogs? To what use could we ever hope to put these great deserts or these great mountain ranges, impenetrable and covered to their base with eternal snow? Mr. President, I will never vote one cent from the public treasury to place the Pacific Coast one inch nearer Boston than it now is.   *Daniel Webster*

JUST THINKING

Men who are the longest remembered, and whose memories are most highly revered, are not those who made

the most money, but those whose hearts were gentle, whose sympathies were broad, and who best served humanity.
Sunshine Magazine

STRENGTH

Sometimes nothing is harder in life than just to endure. There are two types of strength. There is the strength of the wind that sways the mighty oak, and there is the strength of the oak that withstands the power of the wind. There is the strength of the locomotive that pulls the heavy train across the bridge, and there is the strength of the bridge that holds up the weight of the train. One is active strength, the other is passive strength. One is the power to keep going, the other is the power to keep still. One is the strength by which we overcome, the other is the strength by which we endure.
Dr. Harold Phillips, Wesleyan Methodist

THE NEED TO BEWARE

We need to beware lest we spend our lives instead of investing them; waste our energies rather than utilizing them; bury our treasures when we should be cultivating them into new life.
George E. Mayo

SIN

He who commits a sin twice, considers it no longer sin.
The Talmud

AGE

Growing old is a personal problem. The social problem is to create a society in which men and women can live out their days engaged in work which they regard as important and good and in which they are respected for their efforts.
Rollin Chambliss, Atlantic Journal

ANY LARGE CITY?

New York — A volcanic crater of blind, confused human forces pushing together and grinding upon each other. This mantrap of gigantic dimensions . . . is as good an example of barbarism as exists.
Frank Lloyd Wright

TREES

I will sing of the bounty of the big trees
They are the green tents of the Almighty.

Henry Van Dyke

MISTLETOE

One of the legends of the mistletoe relates that it was once a tree but because its wood was used for the cross it shrank in size and became a parasite. Old time monks called the mistletoe the "wood of the cross." It was hung in homes during seasons of gladness, and people kissed each other beneath it because it brought good fortune so long as it was overhead and not underfoot. *Davey Tree Trails*

MAN

The last and best lesson of history is that man is tough. He has survived a thousand catastrophes, and will survive these that encompass him now. Even when the sky falls upon him (as almost literally in modern war), he finds some way to protect himself, some hole in which to hide; and when the evil moment is past, he lifts himself out of the debris of his home, his city, or his civilization, brushes off the dirt, wipes away the blood, and marches on. Somewhere, somehow, he will build again. *Will Durant*

VALUABLE OR DANGEROUS

The past is valuable as a guidepost, but dangerous if used as a hitching post.

GOVERNMENT

All free governments are managed by the combined wisdom and folly of the people. *James A. Garfield*

PRAYER

Prayer does not change God, but changes him who prays.

Soren Kierkegaard

WORK

How do I work? I grope. *Albert Einstein*

COMMON SENSE

Common sense is the measure of the possible.
Frederic Amiel

NO PATH

Too many of us know the short cuts, and too few know or care where the path leads. Too few of us dare to leave the path, because the path is always the easy way, the way most people go. But there is no path to the future, no path to greatness, no path to progress. No path to outer space or to inner satisfaction. *Charles H. Brower*

EDUCATION

Public education is a great instrument of social change. Through it, if we so desire, we can make our country more nearly a democracy without classes. . . . Education is a social process, perhaps the most important process in determining the future of our country; it should command a far larger portion of our national income than it does today.
James B. Conant

WISE-POWERFUL-RICH

Who is wise? He that learns from everyone. Who is powerful? He that governs his passions. Who is rich? He that is content. *Benjamin Franklin*

JUVENILE DELINQUENCY

The deep, underlying cause of delinquent children is simply delinquent adults. There are many contributing causes of delinquency, but only one that is profoundly difficult to cure: the immaturity, the indifference, the lack of moral values on the part of adults delinquent children see every day of their lives. *Eleanor H. Lake, Junior League Mag.*

HOUSE-CLEANING FUN

House cleaning takes so many hours, no matter how I plan, I find old letters to reread, stored magazines to scan.

Old snapshots bring a sigh and smile, though tasks are half undone — it's the old dreams I chance upon that makes house cleaning fun.

OBEDIENCE

Obedience is not the mark of a slave — it is an important quality in leadership. The great leaders of this world have not been their own masters; they arose and followed some-one higher up, and thereby became the greater. Obedience is a gateway to power. Our physical health depends upon obeying the laws of our physical nature. Strength of character issues from obedience to the decree of conscience. If we are to have a commanding hold on life, we must be subject to a will higher than our own.   *The Uplift*

IRONY

It is one of the ironies of life that when one grows tall enough to reach the jam on the pantry shelf, the craving for jam has left.   *Purdue Agriculturist*

AMERICA

In the United States there is more space where nobody is than where anybody is. This is what makes America what she is.   *Gertrude Stein*

With all its faults, America is still the great hope of man-kind. The common people discovered it before the social scientists. The social scientists think of America as a prob-lem. The common people think it is an opportunity.

Dr. Paul Austin Wolfe

ANGER

Anger is a wind which blows out the lamp of the mind.

Robert Ingersoll

THE HEN

A hen keeps on digging worms and laying eggs, re-gardless of "conditions." If the ground is hard, she scratches harder. If it is dry, she digs deeper. If she strikes rock, she works around it. But always she digs up worms and turns them into hard-shelled profits. . . . She saves her breath for digging and her cackle for eggs.   *Rotary Bulletin*

YOURS

What you have in this world will be found on the day of your death to belong to others; what you are will be yours forever.   *Henry Van Dyke*

WE ALREADY HAVE IT

The manager of a department store put this notice in the window: "If you need it, we have it."

But in the window of a rival, a sign appeared stating: "If we don't have it, you don't need it."

PRECEPTS

Here are a few homely precepts which everyone should repeat until they are memorized:

"You may give until you are rich, and you may keep until you are poor.

"Doing nothing except for one's self is the undoing of one's self.

"Do not blame God for the harvest when you yourself do the sowing.

"You cannot whiten yourself by blackening others.

"Religion is not a thing of dispute, but of experience.

"You cannot possibly do good without being made better."
    The Little Visitor

TREES

I think that I shall never see along the road an unmarred tree, with bark intact, and painted white, that no car ever hit at night. For every tree that's near the road has caused some auto to be towed.

Sideswiping trees is done a lot by drivers who are plum halfshot. God gave them eyes so they might see, yet any fool can hit a tree.

Inland Tips, with apologies to the lamented Joyce Kilmer

MAN TO MAN

I had a friend, I loaned him "five." I wonder if he is still alive! Had another, I loaned him "ten." I haven't seen my friend since then! For one more friend I signed a "note." He disappeared and got my goat!

Since man to man is so unjust, I don't know now which man to trust!

FAITH, HOPE, AND CHARITY

Patriotism isn't marching behind a band and puffing out your chest. Patriotism isn't a flash of fireworks one day of the year, and then submerging one's emotions the rest of the year. Patriotism isn't found in the whooping of the crowd or maudlin flag-waving.

Patriotism is the sum of the three cardinal virtues: Faith, Hope, and Charity. Faith in the principles of our government; Hope in the future of our country; Charity toward all and malice toward none.

Patriotism is that spirit that makes us help our neighbors when they are in distress, and extend sympathy when they are stricken.

Patriotism is the tugging at our heartstrings, and a sincere kinship with those who toil in field or shop or marketplace.

Patriotism is the emotion that makes a lump rise in the throat when some intrepid spirit strives to achieve something that no human being ever before achieved.

Patriotism is to be unashamed at the moisture that comes welling up in our tear-ducts with the passing of some great and noble soul, who unselfishly devoted his life to the cause of mankind.

Patriotism is loving one's country, respecting its traditions, and honoring its people, high or low, rich or poor.

Patriotism is standing firm and unselfish for the right, for the common good, for the peace and well-being of all; sacrificing self, if need be, and standing tall and unafraid against all opposition.   *The U. C. A. Lantern*

WHY?

Why is it when I work all day, with no time out for talk or play, my boss is always far away? But every time I stop

to chat, there's Mr. Bossman with his hat. It isn't often that
I shirk — why can't he come when I'm at work?

TWO PROVERBS

If we have no faith in ourselves, and in the kind of future
we can create together, we are fit to follow, not to lead. Let
us remember that the Bible contains two proverbs we cannot
afford to forget. The first is, "Man does not live by bread
alone," and the second is, "Where there is no vision, the
people perish." *Charles Luckman*

ADVICE

Sign on a Beauty Shop: "If your hair isn't becoming to
you, you should be coming to us."

FAITH

Blessings on thee, little man, barefoot boy with cheeks of
tan, trudging down a dusty lane with no thought of future
pain. You're our one and only bet to absorb our National
Debt.

Little man with cares so few, we've got lots of faith in you.
Guard every merry whistled tune, you are apt to need it
soon. Have your fun, boy, while you can, you may be a barefoot man!

AN IDEA

"No," said the little girl's mother. "I don't want you to
hit back at Johnny — you're a lady. Out-talk him."

RIGHT

Only a handful of our forefathers came over in the
"Mayflower," but we're all in the same boat now.

ONE WAY

One Sunday morning a man entered the church and sat
down near the front with his hat on. Noting the man, one
of the ushers spoke to him, asking him if he knew he forgot

to remove his hat. "Yes," the man replied, "I realize I have my hat on but I've been coming to this church for two months, and this is the only way I could get anyone to speak to me."

EVIL TIMES

What would you say was the date of these words:
"We have fallen on evil times, and the world has grown very wicked. Governments are corrupt, and even children are no longer respectful to their parents."

It might be the modern cynic speaking. It might be your scoffing neighbor. But it was not. It is from a clay tablet in a museum in Istanbul (Constantinople), Turkey, and it is dated about 3,000 years B. C.   *Lockport Baptist News*

FLYING THE TRUE COLORS

There are two kinds of great men. Some, by the sheer brilliance of their intellectual genius, are lifted to great heights; but others, much less highly endowed, find greatness in another way. They perceive in their generation the movements of thought and life to which the future belongs, identify themselves with them and stand for them.

The first kind of greatness, individual brilliance, is the gift of destiny to a very few. The second kind of greatness, identifying oneself with the movements of one's time, is open to all. If a cause is to have success, it must have witnesses who will speak up for it and be devoted to it.

Some flagstaffs are very tall and prominent, and some are small, but the glory of a flagstaff is not its size; it is the colors that it flies. A very small flagstaff flying the true colors is far more valuable than a very tall one with false colors. When a man is done with life, I should suppose that the most satisfying thing would be the ability to say, "I may be a-shamed that I was not a better, taller, straighter flagstaff, but I am not ashamed of the colors that I flew."

Harry Emerson Fosdick, American clergyman

NO TRANQUILIZERS

In the good old days nobody needed tranquilizers. There was something else to make you sleep — they called it hard work.

SAY IT —

When you've got a thing to say, say it — don't take half a day; life is short, a fleeting vapor — don't you fill the entire paper with a tale, which at a pinch, could be cornered in an inch. Boil her down until she simmers. Polish her until she glimmers.

When you've got a thing to say, say it — don't take half a day.

POLITICS

Politics has got so expensive that it takes lots of money to even get beat with.   *Will Rogers*

MAYBE

Drive-in banks were established so that cars could see their real owners.

ANYONE KNOW?

Does anyone know where "Sam Hill" is? Or how many feet there are in a far cry? Or the altitude of "It's high time"?

GREAT MINDS

How can great minds be produced in a country where the test of great minds is agreeing with the opinion of small minds?   *John Stuart Mill*

GOVERNMENT

I personally don't believe that any nation should have any national debt. Seems to me, on the other hand, that a great nation like the U. S. should, in all its years of existence, have made a little money instead of having got over $300 billion in debt. A private corporation in business that long and that much in the red would figure it had done a pretty poor job. Even my little granddaughter, Muffie, has $9.16 in her piggie bank. Looks as if the U. S. could have piled up at least $15 or $20 on the asset side in all these years.

Don Herold, quoted in Industrial Press Service

LONGEVITY

A man on his one-hundreth birthday was asked the secret of his longevity. "Just takin' the gifts of the Creator," he answered. "He made the night for sleeping, the day for resting!"

Rev. David A. MacLennan, Church Management

PROGRESS

Aristotle said that all creative people are dissatisfied because they are all looking for happiness in perfection and seeking for things that do not exist. This is one of the hopes of the world. There is no progress where people are satisfied. Discontent is perhaps the most potent challenge to improvement. *Clarence Edwin Flynn, D. D.*

INTERESTING, BUT IS IT TRUE?

Children reared with meticulous care often turn out as well as those permitted to grow up naturally.

Oren Arnold

MOTHER

If they learn nothing else, I want my boys to learn to be thoughtful to their mother — not just to love her, that's easy — but to think about sparing her. Too many boys grow up to think of mother as somebody to wait on them, an attitude that probably carries over when they eventually marry. *Rex Gogerty, Farm Journal*

PERPETUAL IGNORANCE

The receipt for perpetual ignorance is: "Be satisfied with your opinions and content with your knowledge."

Elbert Hubbard

TEACHERS

To teach a bright pupil, get out of his way. It takes a bright teacher to keep far enough ahead of a bright child that the child won't stumble over him in the process.

Mississippi Educational Advance

CHAPTER VII

PERTINENT QUOTATIONS FROM LITERATURE

ACTION

Did nothing in particular
And did it very well.   *W. S. Gilbert*
Heaven ne'er helps the men who will not act. *Sophocles*

ADMIRATION

Admiration is a very short-lived passion, that immediately decays upon growing familiar with its object.
Joseph Addison

ADVERSITY

There is no education like adversity.
Benjamin Disraeli
Prosperity is a great teacher; adversity is a greater. Possession pampers the mind; privation trains and strengthens it.   *William Hazlitt*

ADVICE

Many receive advice, only the wise profit by it.
Publius Syrus
Admonish your friends privately, but praise them openly.
Publius Syrus

AFFECTATION

Affectation is the product of falsehood.
Thomas Carlyle

AFFLICTION

The eternal stars shine out as soon as it is dark enough,
Thomas Carlyle

Be still, sad heart, and cease repining,
Behind the clouds the sun is shining;
Thy fate is the common fate of all;
Into each life some rain must fall, —
Some days must be dark and dreary.

Henry W. Longfellow

AGE

At 20 years of age the will reigns; at 30 the wit; at 40 the judgment. *Benjamin Franklin*

If wrinkles must be written upon our brows, let them not be written upon the heart. The spirit should not grow old.

James A. Garfield

The riders in a race do not stop short when they reach the goal. There is a little finishing canter before coming to a standstill. There is time to hear the kind voice of friends and to say to one's self: "The work is done."

Oliver W. Holmes II

The old believe everything: the middle-aged suspect everything: the young know everything. *Oscar Wilde*

AGRICULTURE

Blessed be agriculture! if one does not have too much of it. *Charles D. Warner*

AMBITION

When you are aspiring to the highest place, it is honorable to reach the second or even the third rank.

Marcus T. Cicero

Ambition destroys its possessor. *The Talmud*

AMERICA

In the United States there is more space where nobody is than where anybody is. This is what makes America what it is. *Gertrude Stein*

American liberty is a religion. It is a thing of the spirit. It is an aspiration on the part of the people for not only a free life but a better life. *Wendell L Willkie*

ANGER

Men often make up in wrath what they want in reason.
W. R. Alger

An angry man opens his mouth and shuts up his eyes.
Marcus P. Cato

ARCHITECTURE

Ah, to build, to build! That is the noblest of all the arts.
Henry W. Longfellow

ARGUE

Wise men argue causes, and fools decide them.
Anacharsis

Never argue at the dinner table, for the one who is not hungry always gets the best of the argument.
Richard Whately

ART

Art is the stored honey of the human soul, gathered on wings of misery and travail.   *Theodore Dreiser*

Great art is as irrational as great music. It is mad with its own loveliness.   *George J. Nathan*

The artist does not see things as they are, but as he is.
Alfred Tonnelle

BIOGRAPHY

Lives of great men all remind us
We can make our lives sublime,
And, departing, leave behind us
Footprints on the sands of time.
Henry W. Longfellow

Every great man nowadays has his disciples, and it is always Judas who writes the biography.   *Oscar Wilde*

BOOKS

All that Mankind has done, thought, gained or been: it is lying as in magic preservation in the pages of Books. They are the chosen possessions of men.   *Thomas Carlyle*

Except a living man there is nothing more wonderful than a book? a message to us from . . . human souls we never saw. . . . And yet these arouse us, terrify us, teach us, comfort us, open their hearts to us as brothers.

Charles Kingsley

BRIBERY

Few men have virtue to withstand the highest bidder.
George Washington

CHARACTER

When wealth is lost, nothing is lost;
When health is lost, something is lost;
When character is lost, all is lost! *Anon.*

Every man has three characters — that which he exhibits, that which he has, and that which he thinks he has.
Alphonse Karr

Not in the clamor of the crowded street,
Not in the shouts and plaudits of the throng,
But in ourselves, are triumph and defeat.
Henry W. Longfellow

CHARITY

You are indeed charitable when you give, and while giving, turn your face away so that you may not see the shyness of the receiver. *Kahlil Gibran*

As the purse is emptied the heart is filled.
Victor Hugo

He— who waits to do a great deal of good at once, will never do anything. *Samuel Johnson*

CHILDHOOD

Teach your child to hold his tongue,
he'll learn fast enough to speak. *Benjamin Franklin*

Children have neither past nor future; and that which seldom happens to us, they rejoice in the present.
Jean de La Bruyere

With little children saying grace
In every Christian kind of place.
Robert L. Stevenson

The best way to make children good is to make them happy. *Oscar Wilde*

CHRISTMAS

O little town of Bethlehem,
How still we see thee lie!
Above thy deep and dreamless sleep
The silent stars go by. *Phillips Brooks*

I heard the bells on Christmas Day
Their old, familiar carols play,
And wild and sweet
The words repeat
Of peace on earth, good-will to men!
Henry W. Longfellow

CHURCH

I never weary of great churches. It is my favorite kind of mountain scenery. Mankind was never so happily inspired as when it made a cathedral.
Robert L. Stevenson

CIRCUMSTANCE

Man is not the creature of circumstances,
Circumstances are the creatures of men.
Benjamin Disraeli

CLERGYMAN

If you would lift me you must be on a higher ground.
Ralph W. Emerson

CLEVERNESS

Cleverness is not wisdom. *Euripides*

COMMUNISM

The theory of Communism may be summed up in one sentence: Abolish all private property.
The Communist Manifesto

CONCEIT

No man was ever so much deceived by another as by himself.   *Sir Fulke Greville*

The art of making much show with little substance.
Thomas B. Macaulay

CONVERSATION

Conversation enriches the understanding, but solitude is the school of genius.   *Edward Gibbon*

COOKING

We may live without friends; we may live without books;
But civilized man cannot live without cooks.
Bulwer-Lytton

COURAGE

Often the test of courage is not to die but to live.
Vittorio Alfieri

Hail, Caesar, those who are about to die salute thee.
Gaius Suetonius

DAY

Think that day lost whose (low) descending sun
Views from thy hand no noble action done.
Jacob Bobart

What a day may bring a day may take away.
Thomas Fuller

DEATH

In the midst of life we are in death.
Book of Common Prayer

Every moment of life is a step towards death.
Pierre Corneille

We begin to die as soon as we are born, and the end is linked to the beginning.   *Manilius*

Till tired, he sleeps, and life's poor play is o'er.
Alexander Pope

To die :-to sleep:
No more; and, by a sleep to say we end
The heart-ache and the thousand natural shocks
That flesh is heir to, 'tis a consummation
Devoutly to be wished.   *William Shakespeare*

DEBT

If you want the time to pass quickly,
just give your note for 90 days.
                              R. B. Thomas

DECEPTION

We are never deceived; we deceive ourselves.
                              Johann Goethe
Hateful to me as are the gates of hell,
Is he who, hiding one thing in his heart,
Utters another.   *Homer*
One is easily fooled by that which one loves. *Moliere*

DECISION

Once to every man and nation comes the moment to
    decide,
In the strife of Truth with Falsehood, for the good or
    evil side.   *James R. Lowell*

DEEDS

We have left undone those things which we ought to
have done; and we have done those things which we ought
not to have done.   *Book of Common Prayer*

DEFEAT

It is defeat that turns bone to flint;
it is defeat that turns gristle to muscle;
it is defeat that makes men invincible.
                              Henry Ward Beecher

DEMOCRACY

When everybody is somebody, then nobody is anybody.
                              Anon.

Democracy arose from men thinking that if they are equal in any respect they are equal in all respects.

Aristotle

The tyranny of a multitude is a multiplied tyranny.

Edmund Burke

I believe in Democracy because it releases the energies of every human being. *Woodrow Wilson*

The world must be made safe for democracy.

Woodrow Wilson

DEMAGOGUE

Demagogues and agitators are very unpleasant, but they are incidents to a free and constitutional country, and you must put up with these inconveniences or do without many important advantages. *Benjamin Disraeli*

DEPENDENCE

People may live as much retired from the world as they please; but sooner or later, before they are aware, they will find themselves debtor or creditor to somebody.

Johann Goethe

He who imagines he can do without the world deceives himself much; but he who fancies the world cannot do without him is still more mistaken.

Francois La Rochefoucauld

DESIRE

Our desires always increase with our possessions. The knowledge that something remains yet unenjoyed impairs our enjoyment of the good before us. *Samuel Johnson*

He who desires naught will always be free.

E. R. Lefebvre Laboulaye

DESTINY

Destiny is not a matter of chance, it is a matter of choice; it is not a thing to be waited for, it is a thing to be achieved.

W. J. Bryan

Every man meets his Waterloo at last.

Wendell Phillips

DIFFICULTY

The three things most difficult are—to keep a secret, to forget an injury, and to make good use of leisure.   *Chilo*

DIGNITY

All celebrated people lose dignity on a close view.
Napoleon Bonaparte

DIPLOMACY

When a diplomat says yes he means perhaps; when he says perhaps he means no; when he says no he is no diplomat.   *Anon.*

DISCONTENT

Who is not satisfied with himself will grow; who is not sure of his own correctness will learn many things.
Chinese Proverb

DOUBT

We know accurately only when we know little, with knowledge doubt increases.   *Johann Goethe*
To be, or not to be, that is the question:
Whether 'tis nobler in the mind to suffer
The slings and arrows of outrageous fortune;
Or to take arms against a sea of troubles,
And by opposing end them?   *William Shakespeare*

DUTY

To do my duty in that state of life unto which it shall please God to call me.   *Book of Common Prayer*
Let us have faith that right makes might, and in that faith let us, to the end, dare to do our duty as we understand it.   *Abraham Lincoln*

EARNESTNESS

Earnestness is the salt of eloquence.   *Victor Hugo*
Earnestness is enthusiasm tempered by reason.
Blaise Pascal

EASTER

Tomb, thou shalt not hold Him longer;
Death is strong, but Life is stronger;
Stronger than the dark, the light
Stronger than the wrong, the right;
Faith and Hope triumphant say
Christ will rise on Easter Day.

Phillips Brooks

"Christ the Lord is risen today,"
Sons of men and angels say.
Raise your joys and triumphs high;
Sing, ye heavens, and earth reply.

Charles Wesley

EDUCATION

Education commences at the mother's knee, and every word spoken within the hearsay of little children tends towards the formation of character. *Hosea Ballou*

The foundation of every state is the education of its youth.
Diogenes

Education is the process of driving a set of prejudices down your throat. *Martin H. Fischer*

There is nothing so stupid as an educated man, if you get off the thing that he was educated in. *Will Rogers*

Education is a companion which no misfortune can depress, no crime can destroy, no enemy can alienate, no despotism can enslave.

At home a friend, abroad an introduction; in solitude a solace and in society an ornament. It chastens vice, it guides virtue, it gives, at once, grace and government to genius. Without it, what is man? A splendid slave, a reasoning savage. *Joseph Addison 1672-1719*

EGOTISM

The reason why lovers are never weary of one another is this — they are always talking of themselves
Francois La Rochefoucauld

ELOQUENCE

Eloquence is the poetry of pros. *William C. Bryant*

Noise proves nothing. Often a hen who has merely laid an egg cackles as if she laid an asteroid.

Samuel L. Clements

ENGLAND

Let us therefore brace ourselves to our duties, and so bear ourselves that, if the British Empire and its Commonwealth last for a thousand years, men will still say. "This was their finest hour."

Winston Churchill

For he might have been a Rooshian
A French or Turk or Proosian,
Or perhaps Italian.
But in spite of all temptations
To belong to other nations,
He remains an Englishman.

W. S. Gilbert

There is nothing so bad or so good that you will not find Englishmen doing it; but you will never find an Englishman in the wrong. He does everything on principle. He fights you on patriotic principles; he robs you on business principles; he enslaves you on imperial principles.

George Bernard Shaw

An Englishman thinks he is moral when he is only uncomfortable.

George Bernard Shaw

ENTHUSIASM

Nothing is so contagious as enthusiasm; it moves stones, it charms brutes. Enthusiasm is the genius of sincerity and truth accomplishes no victories without it.

Edward Bulwer-Lytton

The sense of this word among the Greek affords the noblest definition of it: enthusiasm signifies God in us.

Mme. de Stael

EPITAPH

A tomb now suffices him for whom the whole world was not sufficient.

Epitaph on Alexander the Great

The body of Benjamin Franklin, Printer, (Like the cover of an old book, its contents torn out and stript of its lettering

and gilding), Lies here, food for worms; But the work shall
not be lost, for it will (as he believed) appear once more
in a new and more elegant edition, revised and corrected by
the author.
Benjamin Franklin — Epitaph of Himself, written in 1728

EQUALITY

We hold these truths to be self-evident: that all men are
created equal; that they are endowed by their Creator with
inalienable rights; that among these are life, liberty and the
pursuit of happiness.   *Thomas Jefferson*

Fourscore and seven years ago, our fathers brought forth
on this continent a new nation, conceived in liberty, and dedi-
cated to the proposition that all men are created equal.
Gettysburg Address

EVENTS

Events of great consequence often spring from trifling
circumstances.   *Livy*

EVIDENCE

Evil often triumphs, but never conquers.
Joseph Roux

The evil that men do lives after them;
The good is oft interred with their bones.
William Shakespeare

EXAMPLE

Lives of great men all remind us
We can make our lives sublime,
And, departing, leave behind us
Footprints on the sands of time.
Henry Wadsworth Longfellow

Children have more need of models than of critics.
Joseph Joubert

EXCELLENCE

If a man has good corn, or wood, or boards, or pigs to
sell, or can make better chairs or knives, crucibles, or church

organs, than anybody else, you will find a broad, hard-beaten road to his house, though it be in the woods.

Ralph Waldo Emerson

EXPERIENCE

Experience is the name men give to their follies or their sorrows.   *Alfred de Musset*

Is there anyone so wise as to learn by the experience of others?   *Voltaire*

FACE

He had a face like a benediction.

Saavedra Cervantes

A countenance more in sorrow than in anger.

William Shakespeare

FAILURE

A failure establishes only this, that our determination to succeed was not strong enough. *Christian Nestell Bovee*

But to him who tries and fails and dies,
I give great honor and glory and tears.

Joaquin Miller

FAITH

Faith is the continuation of reason. *William Adams*

An outward and visible sign of an inward and spiritual grace.   *Book of Common Prayer*

All I have seen teaches me to trust the Creator for all I have not seen.   *Ralph Waldo Emerson*

Let us have faith that right makes might; and in that faith, let us, to the end, dare to do our duty as we understand it.   *Abraham Lincoln*

I can believe anything, provided it is incredible.

Oscar Wilde

FAME

If you would not be forgotten as soon as you are dead, either write things worth reading or do things worth writing.   *Benjamin Franklin*

Fame is but the breath of the people, and that often unwholesome.   *Jean J. Rousseau*

FAMILIARITY

Familiarity breeds contempt.   *Anon*
Though familiarity may not breed contempt, it takes off the edge of admiration.   *William Hazlitt*

FARMING

Those who labor in the earth are the chosen people of God, if He ever had a chosen people, whose breasts He has made His peculiar deposit for substantial and genuine virtue.   *Thomas Jefferson*
Farming is a most senseless pursuit, a mere laboring in a circle, You sow that you may reap, and then you reap that you may sow. Nothing ever comes of it.
Johannes Stobaeus

FASHION

A fashionable woman is always in love — with herself.
Francois La Rochefoucauld
I see that the fashion wears out more apparel than the man.   *William Shakespeare*
Fashion is a form of ugliness so intolerable that we have to alter it every six months.   *Oscar Wilde*

FATE

We make our fortunes and we call them fate.
Benjamin Disraeli

"Tis Fate that flings the dice,
And as she flings
Of kings makes peasants,
And of peasants kings.   *John Dryden*

The Moving Finger writes; and having writ,
Moves on; nor all your Piety not Wit
Shall lure it back to cancel half a Line,
Nor all your Tears wash out a Word of it.
Omar Khayyam

FATHER

A father is a banker provided by nature.

French Proverb

The child is father of the man.

William Wordsworth

FAULT

The greatest of faults, I should say, is to be conscious of none. *Thomas Carlyle*

The defects of great men are the consolation of the dunces. *Isaac D'Israeli*

We keep on deceiving ourselves in regard to our faults, until we at last come to look upon them as virtues.

Henrich Heine

FEAR

Fear always springs from ignorance.

Ralph Waldo Emerson

The meek, the terrible meek, the fierce agonizing meek, are about to enter into their inheritance.

Charles R. Kennedy

From a distance it is something; and nearby it is nothing.

Jean de La Fontaine

They are slaves who fear to speak
For the fallen and the weak. *James Russell Lowell*

FIRMNESS

That which is called firmness in a king is called obstinancy in a donkey. *Lord Erskine*

FISHING

A fishing-rod was a stick with a hook at one end and a fool at the other. *Samuel Johnson*

We may say of angling as Dr. Boteler said of strawberries: "Doubtless God could have made a better berry, but doubtless God never did"; and so, (if I might be judge,) God never did make a more calm, quiet, innocent recreation than angling. *Izaak Walton*

FLAG

When Freedom from her mountain height
Unfurled her standard to the air,
She wore the azure robe of night,
And set the stars of glory there.   *Joseph R. Drake*

Let it rise! let it rise, till it meet the sun in his coming:
let the earliest light of the morning gild it, and the parting
day linger and play on its summit.   *Daniel Webster*

FLATTERY

Men are like stone jugs — you may lug them where you
like by the ears.   *Samuel Johnson*

It is easy to flatter; it is harder to praise.
                    Jean Paul Richter

O, that men's ears should be
To counsel deaf, but not to flattery!
                    William Shakespeare

FLEA

Great fleas have little fleas upon their
    backs to bite 'em,
And little fleas have lesser fleas, and
    so ad infinitum.
And the great fleas themselves, in
    turn, have greater fleas to go on;
While these again have greater still,
    and greater still, and so on.

                    Augustus De Morgan

FLOWERS

Flowers have an expression of countenace as much as men
or animals. Some seem to smile; some have a sad expression; some are pensive and diffident; others again are plain,
honest and upright, like the broad-faced sunflower and the
hollyhock.
                    Henry Ward Beecher

The buttercups, bright-eyed and bold,
Held up their chalices of gold
To catch the sunshine and the dew.

Julia C. R. Dorr

In Flanders' field the poppies grow
Between the crosses, row on row,
That mark our place, and in the sky,
The larks, still bravely singing, fly
Scarce heard among the guns below.

John McCrae

One thing is certain and the rest is lies;
The Flower that once has blown for ever dies.

Omar Khayyam

To me the meanest flower that blows can give
Thoughts that do often lie too deep for tears.

William Wordsworth

FOLLY

The folly of one man is the fortune of another.

Francis Bacon

He has spent all his life in letting down empty buckets
into empty wells, and he is frittering away his age in trying
to draw them up again.   *Sydney Smith*

FOOL

Young men think old men are fools; but old men know
young men are fools.   *George Chapman*

Hain't we got all the fools in town on our side? And
ain't that a big enough majority in any town?

Samuel L. Clemens

Nobody can describe a fool to the life, without much
patient self-inspection.   *Frank M. Colby*

A learned fool is more foolish than an ignorant fool.

Moliere

He who thinks himself wise, O heavens! is a great fool.

Voltaire

FORGETFULNESS

There is no remembrance which time does not obliterate,
nor pain which death does not terminate.

Saavedra Cervantes

The pyramids themselves, doting with age, have forgotten the names of the founders.

> God of our fathers, known of old,
> Lord of our far-flung battle-line,
> Beneath whose awful Hand we hold
> Dominion over palm and pine —
> Lord God of Hosts, be with us yet,
> Lest we forget — lest we forget!
>
> The tumult and the shouting dies,
> The captains and the kings depart;
> Still stands thine ancient sacrifice,
> A humble and a contrite heart.
> Lord God of Hosts, be with us yet,
> Lest we forget — lest we forget.
>
> *Rudyard Kipling*

Who is the Forgotten Man? He is the calm, quiet, virtuous, domestic citizen, who pays his debts and his taxes and is never heard of out of his little circle.

William G. Summer

FORGIVENESS

God pardons like a mother, who kisses the offense into everlasting forgetfulness.   *Henry Ward Beecher*

To err is human, to forgive, divine.   *Alexander Pope*

It is manlike to punish but godlike to forgive.

Peter von Winter

FOX

A sleeping fox counts hens in his dreams.

Russian Proverb

FREEDOM

The cause of freedom is the cause of God.

Samuel Bowles

Personal liberty is the paramount essential to human dignity and human happiness.

Edward Bulwer-Lytton

In a free country there is much clamor, with little suffering; in a despotic state there is little complaint, with much grievance.

Hippolyte L. Carnot

Freedom suppressed and again regained bites with keener fangs than freedom never endangered.

Marcus T. Cicero

I am for freedom of religion and against all maneuvers to bring about a legal ascendancy of one sect over another.

Thomas Jefferson

. . . That this nation, under God, shall have a new birth of freedom. *Abraham Lincoln*

The only freedom which deserves the name is that of pursuing our own good in our own way, so long as we do not attempt to deprive others of theirs or impede their efforts to obtain it. *John Stuart Mill*

FRIEND

Prosperity makes friends and adversity tries them.

Anon

A friend must not be injured, even in jest.

Publius Syrus

Reprove your friends in secret, praise them openly.

Publius Syrus

GENIUS

The poets' scrolls will outlive the monuments of stone. Genius survives; all else is claimed by death.

Edmund Spenser

GIFT

You give but little when you give of your possessions. It is when you give of yourself that you truly give.

Kahlil Gibran

GLORY

The paths of glory lead but to the grave.

Thomas Gray

O how quickly passes away the glory of the earth.

Thomas A. Kempis

GOD

God moves in a mysterious way
His wonders to perform;
He plants his footsteps in the sea
And rides upon the storm.   *William Cowper*

GOLDEN RULE

My duty towards my neighbor is to love him as myself,
and to do to all men as I would they should do unto me.
Book of Common Prayer

GOSSIP

There is only one thing in the world worse than being
talked about, and that is not being talked about.
Oscar Wilde

GOVERNMENT

Experience teaches us to be most on our guard to protect
liberty when the government's purposes are beneficent.
Louis D. Brandeis

I think we have more machinery of government than is
necessary, too many parasites living on the labor of the
industrious.   *Thomas Jefferson*

Republics end through luxury; monarchies through
poverty.   *Charles de Secondat Montesquieu*

The labor unions shall have a square deal, and the
corporations shall have a square deal, and in addition, all
private citizens shall have a square deal.
Theodore Roosevelt

GRATITUDE

He who receives a good turn should never forget it; he
who does one should never remember it.
Pierre Charron

Gratitude is the heart's memory.   *French Proverb*

GREATNESS

No man ever yet became great by imitation.
Samuel Johnson

It is the prerogative of great men only to have great
defects.   *Francois La Rochefoucauld*

HEART

Still stands thine ancient sacrifice —
An humble and a contrite heart.   *Rudyard Kipling*

No one is so accursed by fate,
No one so utterly desolate,
But some heart, though unknown,
Responds unto his own.
                          Henry Wadsworth Longfellow

HERO

Hero-worship exists, has existed, and will forever exist,
universally among mankind.   *Thomas Carlyle*
The idol of today pushes the hero of yesterday out of
our recollection; and will, in turn, be supplanted by his suc-
cessor of tomorrow.   *Washington Irving*

HISTORY

There is properly no history, only biography.
                          Ralph Waldo Emerson
History is indeed little more than the register of the
crimes, follies, and misfortunes of mankind.
                                 Edward Gibbon
The historian is a prophet looking backwards.
                              August W. Schlegel

HOME

A man travels the world over in search of what he needs
and returns home to find it.   *George Moore*
Home is where the heart is.   *Gaius Pliny*

HONOR

For Brutus is an honourable man;
So are they all, all honourable men.   —
                              William Shakespeare

The nation's honor is dearer than the nation's comfort; yes, than the nation's lift itself.   *Woodrow Wilson*

HUMANITY

Humanity is the Son of God.   *Theodore Parker*
For the interesting and inspiring thing about America, gentlemen, is that she asks nothing for herself except what she has a right to ask for humanity itself.
Woodrow Wilson

HUMILITY

Humility is the solid foundation of all the virtues.
Confucius
I believe the first test of a truly great man is his humility.
John Ruskin

HUSBAND

All husbands are alike, but they have different faces so you can tell them apart.   *Anon.*

IDEAS

No army can withstand the strength of an idea whose time has come.   *Victor Hugo*

IGNORANCE

Ignorance is the mother of fear.   *Henry Home*
Imagination disposes of everything; it creates beauty, justice, and happiness, which is everything in this world.
Blaise Pascal
Imagination is the eye of the soul.   *Joseph Joubert*

IMMORTALITY

What is human is immortal! *Edward Bulwer-Lytton*
I have been dying for twenty years, now I am going to live.   *James Drummond Burns*
A good man never dies.   *Callimachus*
The nearer I approach the end, the plainer I hear around me the immortal symphonies of the world which invite me. It is marvelous, yet simple.   *Victor Hugo*

There is no death! the stars go down
To rise upon some fairer shore.   *J. L. McCreery*

JOY

For human joys are swift of wing,
For Heaven doth so allot it;
That when you get an easy thing,
You find you haven't got it.   *Eugene Field*

KNOWLEDGE

Strange how much you've got to know
Before you know how little you know.   *Anon.*

Our knowledge is the amassed thought and experience of
innumerable minds.   *Ralph W. Emerson*

We know what we are, but I know not what we may be.
     William Shakespeare

LABOR

He who prays and labours lifts his heart to God with
his hands.   *St. Bernard*

Labor, if it were not necessary for the existence, would
be indispensable for the happiness of man.
     Samuel Johnson

LEARNING

And still they gazed, and still the wonder grew,
That one small head should carry all it knew.
     Oliver Goldsmith

LIFE

Every man's life is a fairy-tale written by God's fingers.
     Hans Christian Andersen

I expect to pass through this world but once. Any good
therefore that I can do, or any kindness that I can show to
any fellow creature, let me do it now. Let me not defer
or neglect it, for I shall not pass this way again.   *Anon.*

One life — a little gleam of Time between two Eternities.
     Thomas Carlyle

LOVE

Greater love hath no man than this, that a man lay down his life for his friends.   *John. XV. 13*

MAN

Let each man think himself an act of God.
His mind a thought, his life a breath of God. *Bailey*
Man passes away; his name perishes from record and recollection; his history is as a tale that is told, and his very monument becomes a ruin.   *Washington Irving*
His life was gentle, and the elements
So mix'd in him that Nature might stand up,
And say to all the world, This was a man.
William Shakespeare

MATRIMONY

Marriage is that relation between man and woman in which the independence is equal, the dependence mutual, and the obligation reciprocal.   *Louis K. Anspacher*
With this ring I thee wed, with my body I thee worship, and with all my wordly goods I thee endow.
Book of Common Prayer

MODESTY

Modesty is the conscience of the body.
Honore de Balzac
Modesty is the only sure bait when you angle for praise.
Lord Chesterfield

MONEY

Make all you can, save all you can, give all you can.
John Wesley

MUSIC

The man that hath no music in himself,
Nor is not moved with concord of sweet sounds,
Is fit for treasons, stratagems and spoils.
William Shakespeare

NEWSPAPER

The careful reader of a few good newspapers can learn
more in a year than most scholars do in their great libraries.

F. B. Sanborn

ORATORY

Oratory is the power to talk people out of their sober
and natural opinions.   *Paul Chatfield*

PATIENCE

Patience is the art of hoping.

Luc de Clapiers Vauvenargues

PESSIMISM

Pessimist: An optimist who endeavored to practice what
he preached.   *Anon.*

POET

A great poet is the most precious jewel of a nation.

Ludwig von Beethoven

No man was ever yet a great poet, without at the same
time being a profound philosopher.

Hartley Coleridge

POLITICS

I always voted at my party's call,
And I never thought of thinking for myself at all.

W. S. Gilbert

As long as I count the votes what are you going to do
about it?   *William M. Tweed*

PRAISE

I praise loudly; I blame softly.

Catherine II of Russia

PRAYER

Between the humble and contrite heart and the majesty
of heaven there are no barriers; the only password is prayer.

Hosea Ballou

A prayer, in its simplest definition, is merely a wish turned heavenward. *Phillips Brooks*

Prayer is the voice of faith. *Richard H. Horne*

PREJUDICE

Prejudice is the child of ignorance. *William Hazlitt*

PRICE

All good things are cheap; all bad are very dear. *Henry David Thoreau*

PRIDE

Pride goeth before destruction, and an haughty spirit before a fall. *Proverbs. XVI. 18*

The infinitely little have a pride infinitely great. *Voltaire*

SELF-PRAISE

If you wish in this world to advance
Your merits you're bound to enhance;
You must stir it and stump it,
And blow your own trumpet,
Or, trust me, you haven't a chance. *W. S. Gilbert*

SILENCE

Keep quiet and people will think you a philosopher. *Latin Proverb*

Blessed are they who have nothing to say, and who cannot be persuaded to say it. *James R. Lowell.*

SORROW

I walked a mile with Sorrow
And ne'er a word said she;
But, oh, the things I learned from her
When Sorrow walked with me. *Robert B. Hamilton*

SPEECH

A sophistical rhetorician, inebriated with the exuberance of his own verbosity. *Benjamin Disraeli*

STATE

A state is a perfect body of free men, united together to enjoy common rights and advantages.

Hugo Grotius

SUCCESS

All you need in this life is ignorance and confidence, and then Success is sure.   *S. L. Clemens*

TALK

But far more numerous was the herd of such,
Who think too little, and who talk too much.

John Dryden

TEACHING

The teacher is like the candle which lights others in consuming itself.   *Giovanni Ruffini*

THOUGHT

Yond Cassius has a lean and hungry look;
He thinks too much: such men are dangerous.

William Shakespeare

Gather ye rose-buds while ye may,
Old Time is still aflying,
And this same flower that smiles today,
Tomorrow will be dying.   *Robert Herrick*

WANT

Man wants but little here below,
Nor wants that little long.   *Oliver Goldsmith*

WAR

War is the greatest plague that can afflict humanity; it destroys religion, it destroys states, it destroys families. Any scourge is preferable to it.   *Martin Luther*

WEATHER

I was born with a chronic anxiety about the weather.
John Burroughs

WICKEDNESS

No man ever became very wicked all at once.
Decimus J. Juvenal

WISDOM

As for me, all I know is that I know nothing.
Socrates

WOMAN

But what is woman? Only one of nature's agreeable blunders. *Abraham Cowley*

Grace was in all her steps, heaven in her eye,
In every gesture dignity and love. *John Milton*

WORK

I never did anything worth doing by accident, nor did any of my inventions come by accident; they came by work.
Thomas Edison

I like work; it fascinates me. I can sit and look at it for hours. I love to keep it by me: the idea of getting rid of it nearly breaks my heart. *Jerome K. Jerome*

Heaven is blessed with prefect rest but the blessing of earth is toil. *Henry Van Dyke*

WORLD

Socrates, indeed, when he was asked of what country he called himself, said, "Of the world"; for he considered himself an inhabitant and a citizen of the whole world.
Cicero

This world is all a fleeting show,
For man's illusion given;
The smiles of joy, the tears of woe,
Deceitful shine, deceitful flow, —
There's nothing true but Heaven. *Thomas Moore*

WRONG

I remember my youth and the feeling that will never come back any more — the feeling that I could last forever, outlast the sea, the earth, and all men.   *Joseph Conrad*

CHAPTER VIII

A TREASURY OF BIBLICAL QUOTATIONS

ABILITY

If ye have faith as a grain of mustard seed . . . nothing shall be impossible unto you. *Matt. 17:20*

All things are possible to him that believeth.
Mark 9:23

I can do all things through Christ which strengtheneth me. *Phil. 4:13*

ABSENT

The Lord watch between me and thee, when we are absent one from another. *Gen. 31:49*

ACHIEVEMENT

I have fought a good fight, I have finished my course, I have kept the faith. *2 Tim. 4:7*

AFFLICTION

Many are the afflictions of the righteous: but the Lord delivereth him out of them all. *Psa. 34:19*

Come unto me, all ye that labour and are heavy laden, and I will give you rest. *Matt. 11:28*

We know that all things work together for good to them that love God, to them who are the called according to his purpose. *Rom. 8:28*

The Lord is my helper, and I will not fear what man shall do unto me. *Heb. 13:6*

AGE

With the ancient is wisdom; and in length of days understanding. *Job 12:2*

We all do fade as a leaf. *Isa. 64:6*

Aged men be sober, grave, temperate, sound in faith, in charity, in patience. *Tit. 2:2*

AMBITION

Seekest thou great things for thyself? seek them not.
Jer. 45:5

What is a man profited, if he shall gain the whole world, and lose his own soul? *Matt. 16:26*

Whosoever will be great among you, shall be your minister: and whosoever of you will be the chiefest, shall be servant of all. *Mark 10:43, 44*

All that is in the world, the lust of the flesh, and the lust of the eyes, and the pride of life, is not of the Father, but is of the world. *I John 2:16*

ANGER

He that is slow to anger is better than the mighty; and he that ruleth his spirit than he that taketh a city.
Prov. 16:32

Let all bitterness, and wrath, and anger, and clamour, and evil speaking, be put away from you, with all malice.
Eph. 4:31

ANXIETY

Yea, though I walk through the valley of the shadow of death, I will fear no evil: for thou art with me; thy rod and thy staff they comfort me. *Psa. 23:4*

Take no thought for your life, what ye shall eat, or what ye shall drink; nor yet for your body, what ye shall put on. Is not the life more than meat, and the body than raiment?
Matt. 6:25

APPEARANCE

Judge not according to the appearance. *John 7:24*

BEATITUDES

Blessed are the poor in spirit: for theirs is the kingdom of heaven. Blessed are they that mourn: for they shall be comforted. Blessed are the meek: for they shall inherit the earth. Blessed are they which do hunger and thirst after righteousness: for they shall be filled. Blessed are the merciful: for they shall obtain mercy. Blessed are the pure in heart: for they shall see God. Blessed are the peace-makers: for they shall be called the children of God. Blessed are they which are persecuted for righteousness' sake: for theirs is the kingdom of heaven. *Matt. 5:3-12*

BEAUTY

Beauty is a fading flower. *Isa. 28:1*

Consider the lilies of the field, how they grow; they toil not, neither do they spin: And yet I say unto you, That even Solomon in all his glory was not arrayed like one of these. *Matt. 6:28, 29*

BEHAVIOR

Whatsoever ye would that men should do to you, do ye even so to them. *Matt. 7:12*

Whether . . . ye eat, or drink, or whatsoever ye do, do all to the glory of God. *I Cor. 10:31*

Be thou an example of the believers, in word, in conversation, in charity, in spirit, in faith, in purity. *I Tim. 4:12*

BENEDICTION

The Lord bless thee, and keep thee: The Lord make his face shine upon thee, and be gracious unto thee: The Lord lift up his countenance upon thee, and give thee peace. *Num. 6:24-26*

BOASTING

Boast not thyself of tomorrow; for thou knowest not what a day may bring forth. *Prov. 27:1*

Let another man praise thee; and not thine own mouth; a stranger, and not thine own lips. *Prov. 27:2*

BODY

Know ye not that ye are the temple of God, and that the Spirit of God dwelleth in you? *I Cor. 3:17*

BROTHERHOOD

Have we not all one father? hath not one God created us? *Mal. 2:10*

Inasmuch as ye have done it unto one of the least of these my brethren, ye have done it unto me.   *Matt. 25:40*

BUSINESS

Seest thou a man diligent in his business? He shall stand before kings.   *Prov. 22:29*

He that had received the five talents went and traded with the same, and made them other five talents.

Matt. 25:16

CARE

Come unto me, all ye that labour and are heavy laden, and I will give you rest.   *Matt. 11:28*

CHARITY

Charity suffereth long, and is kind; charity envieth not; charity vaunteth not itself, is not puffed up, Doth not behave itself unseemly, seeketh not her own, is not easily provoked, thinketh no evil; Rejoiceth not in iniquity, but rejoiceth in the truth; Beareth all things, believeth all things, hopeth all things, endureth all things.

I Cor. 13:4-7

Be ye kind one to another, tenderhearted, forgiving one another, even as God for Christ's sake hath forgiven you.

Eph. 4:32

Be thou an example of the believers, in word, in conversation, in charity.   *I Tim. 4:12*

Speak evil of no man.   *Tit. 3:2*

CHILDREN

Train up a child in the way he should go: and when he is old, he will not depart from it.   *Prov. 22:6*

When I was a child, I spake as a child, I understood as a child, I thought as a child: but when I became a man, I put away childish things.   *I Cor. 13:11*

CHOICE

I have set before you life and death, blessing and cursing: therefore choose life, that both thou and thy seed may live.

Deut. 30:19

Choose you this day whom ye will serve. *Josh. 24:15*
How long halt ye between two opinions? if the Lord be God, follow him; but if Baal, then follow him.

I Kin. 18:21

CHRIST

The Son of man came not to be ministered unto, but to minister, and to give his life a ransom for many.

Matt. 20:28

I am the way, the truth, and the life.   *John 14:6*

CHURCH

Mine house shall be called a house of prayer for all people.   *Isa. 56:7*
Upon this rock I will build my church; and the gates of hell shall not prevail against it.   *Matt. 16:18*

COMFORT

The eternal God is thy refuge, and underneath are the everlasting arms.   *Deut. 33:27*
In the day when I cried thou answeredst me, and strengthenedst me with strength in my soul. *Psa. 138.3*
I, even I, am he that comforteth you: who art thou, that thou shouldest be afraid of a man that shall die, and of the son of man which shall be made as grass. *Isa. 51:12*
I will never leave thee, nor forsake thee. *Heb. 13:5*

CONCEIT

Be not wise in thine own eyes.   *Prov. 3:5*
Woe unto them that are wise in their own eyes, and prudent in their own sight!   *Isa. 5:21*
Let not the wise man glory in his wisdom, neither let the mighty man glory in his might, let not the rich man glory in his riches.   *Jer. 9:23*
If a man think himself to be something, when he is nothing, he deceiveth himself.   *Gal. 6:3*

CONSCIENCE

As he thinketh in his heart, so is he.   *Prov. 23:7*

COURAGE

Be strong and of good courage. *Deut. 31:6*

The Lord is my light and my salvation; whom shall I fear? the Lord is the strength of my life; of whom shall I be afraid? *Psa. 27:1*

Be of good courage, and he shall strengthen your heart, all ye that hope in the Lord. *Psa. 31:24*

If God be for us, who can be against us? *Rom. 8:31*

Watch ye, stand fast in the faith, quit you like men, be strong. *I Cor. 16:13*

DEATH

Lord, make me to know mine end, and the measure of my days, what it is; that I may know how frail I am.
Psa. 39:4

Teach us to number our days that we may apply our hearts unto wisdom. *Psa. 90:12*

Then shall the dust return to the earth as it was: and the spirit shall return unto God who gave it. *Eccl. 12:7*

We know that if our earthly house of this tabernacle were dissolved, we have a building of God, a house not made with hands, eternal in the heavens. *2 Cor. 5:1*

We brought nothing into this world, and it is certain we can carry nothing out. *I Tim. 6:7*

DESPAIR

When my soul fainted within me I remembered the Lord.
Jonah 2:7

We are perplexed, but not in despair. *2 Cor. 4:8*

DUTY

Fear God, and keep his commandments: for this is the whole duty of man. *Eccl. 12:13*

What doth the Lord require of thee, but to do justly, and to love mercy, and to walk humbly with thy God?
Mic. 6:8

We then that are strong ought to bear the infirmities of the weak, and not to please ourselves. *Rom. 15:1*

ENMITY

Rejoice not when thine enemy falleth, and let not thine heart be glad when he stumbleth. *Prov. 24:17*

Love your enemies, bless them that curse you, do good to them that hate you, and pray for them which despitefully use you, and persecute you. *Matt. 5:44*

If ye forgive men their trespasses, your heavenly Father will also forgive you. *Matt. 6:14*

If thine enemy hunger, feed him; if he thirst, give him drink: for in so doing thou shalt heap coals of fire on his head. *Rom. 12:20*

ETERNITY

Before the mountains were brought forth, or ever thou hadst formed the earth and the world, even from everlasting to everlasting, thou art God. *Psa. 90:2*

EVIL

A good man out of the good treasure of the heart bringeth forth good things: and an evil man out of the evil treasure bringeth forth evil things. *Matt. 12:35*

EXAMPLE

Let your light so shine before men, that they may see your good works, and glorify your Father which is in heaven. *Matt. 5:16*

I have given you an example, that ye should do as I have done to you. *John 13:15*

FAITH

Commit thy way unto the Lord; trust also in him; and he shall bring it to pass. *Psa. 37:5*

Blessed is that man that maketh the Lord his trust. *Psa. 40:4*

What time I am afraid, I will trust in thee. *Psa. 56:3*

All things, whatsoever ye shall ask in prayer, believing, ye shall receive. *Matt. 21:22*

Faith without works is dead. *Jas. 2:20*

FALSEHOOD

Thou shalt not bear false witness against thy neighbour.
Ex. 20:16

Ye shall not steal, neither deal falsely, neither lie one to another. *Lev. 19:11*

FLATTERY

The poor is hated even of his own neighbour: but the rich hath many friends. *Prov. 14:20*

Many will intreat the favour of the prince: and every man is a friend to him that giveth gifts. *Prov. 19:6*

FOOL

The way of a fool is right in his own eyes: but he that hearkeneth unto counsel is wise. *Prov. 12:15*

A fool's mouth is his destruction, and his lips are the snare of his soul. *Prov. 18:7*

FORGIVENESS

If thine enemy be hungry, give him bread to eat; and if he be thirsty, give him water to drink. *Prov. 25:21*

If ye forgive men their trespasses, your heavenly Father will also forgive you. *Matt. 6:14*

Why beholdest thou the mote that is in thy brother's eye, but considerest not the beam that is in thine own eye?
Matt. 7:3

FRIENDSHIP

A friend loveth at all times, and a brother is born for adversity. *Prov. 17:17*

Greater love hath no man than this, that a man lay down his life for his friends. *John 15:13*

GIVING

He that hath pity upon the poor lendeth unto the Lord; and that which he hath given will he pay him again.
Prov. 19:17

Take heed that ye do not your alms before men, to be

seen of them . . . But when thou doest alms, let not thy left hand know what thy right hand doeth.

Matt. 6:1, 3

Give, and it shall be given unto you; good measure, pressed down, and shaken together, and running over.

Luke 6:38

It is more blessed to give than to receive. *Acts 20:35*

GOD

The eternal God is thy refuge, and underneath are the everlasting arms. *Deut. 33:27*

The Lord seeth not as man seeth; for man looketh on the outward appearance, but the Lord looketh on the heart.

I Sam. 16:7

In whose hand is the soul of every living thing, and the breath of all mankind. *Job 12:10*

The fool hath said in his heart, There is no God.

Psa. 14:1

The Lord is good; his mercy is everlasting; and his truth endureth to all generations. *Psa. 100:5*

God is no respecter of persons. *Acts 20:34*

There is one God, the Father, from whom are all things and for whom we exist.

I Cor. 8:6

GOODNESS

Whatsoever things are true, whatsoever things are honest, whatsoever things are just, whatsoever things are pure, whatsoever things are lovely, whatsoever things are of good report; if there be any virtue, and if there be any praise, think on these things. *Phil. 4:8*

GOSSIP

Thou shalt not go up and down as a talebearer among thy people. *Lev. 19:16*

GREED

Better is a little with righteousness than great revenues without right. *Prov. 16:8*

HARVEST

Every good tree bringeth forth good fruit; but a corrupt tree bringeth forth evil fruit. *Matt. 7:17*

Whatsoever a man soweth, that shall he also reap.
Gal. 6:7

HATRED

Love your enemies, bless them that curse you, do good to them that hate you, and pray for them which despitefully use you, and persecute you. *Matt. 5:44*

He that loveth not his brother abideth in death.
I John 3:14

HEART

The Lord seeth not as man seeth; for man looketh on the outward appearance, but the Lord looketh on the heart.
Sam. 16:7

Create in me a clean heart, O God; and renew a right spirit within me. *Psa. 51:10*

Blessed are the pure in heart: for they shall see God.
Matt. 5:8

HEAVEN

Lay up for yourselves treasures in heaven, where neither moth nor rust doth corrupt, and where thieves do not break through nor steal. *Matt. 6:20*

God shall wipe away all tears from their eyes; and there shall be no more death, neither sorrow, nor crying, neither shall there be any more pain: for the former things are passed away. *Rev. 21:4*

HOPE

Be of good courage, and he shall strengthen your heart, all ye that hope in the Lord. *Psa. 31:24*

The eye of the Lord is upon them that fear him, upon them that hope in his mercy. *Psa. 33:18*

Blessed is the man that trusteth in the Lord, and whose hope the Lord is. *Jer. 17:7*

HUMILITY

What doth the Lord require of thee, but to . . . walk humbly with Thy God?   *Mic. 6:8*

Whosoever therefore shall humble himself as this little child, the same is greatest in the kingdom of heaven.
Matt. 18:4

Whosoever will be great among you, let him be your minister; And whosoever will be chief among you, let him be your servant.   *Matt. 20:26, 27*

Whosoever shall exalt himself shall be abased; and he that shall humble himself shall be exalted. *Matt. 23:12*

God forbid that I should glory, save in the cross of our Jesus Christ.   *Gal. 6:14*

HYPOCRISY

Take heed that ye do not your alms before men, to be seen of them: otherwise ye have no reward of your Father which is in heaven.   *Matt. 6:1*

No man can serve two masters: for either he will hate the one, and love the other; or else he will hold to the one, and despise the other. Ye cannot serve God and mammon.
Matt. 6:24

Thou hypocrite, first cast out the beam out of thine own eye; and then shalt thou see clearly to cast out the mote out of thy brother's eye.   *Matt. 7:5*

Though I speak with the tongues of men and of angels, and have not charity, I am become as sounding brass, or a tinkling cymbal.   *I Cor. 13:1*

IDLENESS

Love not sleep, lest thou come to poverty.
Prov. 20:13

Drowsiness shall clothe a man with rags.
Prov. 23:21

IGNORANCE

Fools despise wisdom and instruction.   *Prov. 1:7*

My people are destroyed for lack of knowledge.
Hos. 4:6

The wisdom of this world is foolishness with God.
I Cor. 3:19

IMMORTALITY

O death, where is thy sting? O grave, where is thy victory? *I Cor. 15:55*

The world passeth away, and the lust thereof: but he that doeth the will of God abideth for ever.
I John 2:17

INDECISION

How long halt ye between two opinions? If the Lord be God, follow him: but if Baal, then follow him.
I Kin. 18:21

INSTRUCTION

The fear of the Lord is the beginning of knowledge: but fools despise wisdom and instruction. *Prov. 1:7*

Wisdom is the principal thing; therefore get wisdom: and with all thy getting get understanding. *Prov. 4:7*

Train up a child in the way he should go: and when he is old, he will not depart from it. *Prov. 22:6*

INTEGRITY

Better is the poor that walketh in his integrity, than he that is perverse in his lips, and is a fool. *Prov. 19:1*

The just man walketh in his integrity: his children are blessed after him. *Prov. 20:7*

JOY

Happy is that people, whose God is the Lord.
Psa. 144:15

Whoso trusteth in the Lord, happy is he.
Prov. 16:20

JUDGMENT

With what judgment ye judge, ye shall be judged: and

with what measure ye mete, it shall be measured to you
again. *Matt. 7:2*

Judge not according to the appearance, but judge righteous judgment. *John 7:24*

He that is without sin among you, let him cast a stone.
John 8:7

JUSTICE

Defend the poor and fatherless; do justice to the afflicted
and needy. *Psa. 82:3*

What doth the Lord require of thee, but to do justly,
and to love mercy, and to walk humbly with thy God?
Mic. 6:8

KINDNESS

If a man be overtaken in a fault, ye which are spiritual,
restore such an one in the spirit of meekness; considering
thyself, lest thou also be tempted. *Gal. 6:1*

As we have therefore opportunity, let us do good unto
all men. *Gal. 6:10*

KNOWLEDGE

The fear of the Lord is the beginning of knowledge.
Prov. 1:7

Wise men lay up knowledge. *Prov. 10:14*

LAW

He that keepeth the law, happy is he. *Prov. 29:18*

This is the love of God, that we keep his commandments.
I John 5:3

LIBERTY

Ye shall know the truth, and the truth shall make you
free. *John 8:32*

Take heed lest by any means this liberty of yours become
a stumbling block to them that are weak. *I Cor. 8:9*

LIFE

All that a man hath will he give for his life. *Job 2:4*

Lord, make me to know mine end, and the measure of my days, what it is; that I may know how frail I am.
Psa. 39:4

He that loveth his life shall lose it. *John 12:25*

None of us liveth to himself, and no man dieth to himself. *Rom. 14:7*

LOVE

Thou shalt love thy neighbor as thyself. *Lev. 19:18*

A friend loveth at all times, and a brother is born for adversity. *Prov. 17:17*

If a man say, I love God, and hateth his brother, he is a liar: for he that loveth not his brother whom he hath seen, how can he love God whom he hath not seen?
I John 4:20

MAN

God created man in his own image. *Gen. 1:27*

Man that is born of woman is of few days, and full of trouble. He cometh forth like a flower, and is cut down: he fleeth also as a shadow, and continueth not. *Job 14:1, 2*

Man is like to vanity: his days are as a shadow that passeth away. *Psa. 144:4*

MARRIAGE

The Lord God said, It is not good that the man should be alone; I will make him an help meet for him.
Gen. 2:18

What therefore God hath joined together, let not man put asunder. *Mark 10:9*

MEDITATION

Whatsoever things are true, whatsoever things are honest, whatsoever things are just, whatsoever things are pure, whatsoever things are lovely, whatsoever things are of good report; if there be any virtue, and if there be any praise, think on these things. *Phil. 4:8*

MEEKNESS

A soft answer turneth away wrath. *Prov. 15:1*

Blessed are the meek: for thy shall inherit the earth.
Matt. 5:5

MERCY

What doth the Lord require of thee, but to do justly, and to love mercy, and to walk humbly with thy God?
Mic. 6:8

Blessed are the merciful: for they shall obtain mercy.
Matt. 5:7

NATURE

In the beginning God created the heaven and the earth.
Gen. 1:1

The flowers appear on the earth; the time of the singing of birds is come. *S. of S. 2:12*

OBEDIENCE

Fear God, and keep his commandments: for this is the whole duty of man. *Eccl. 12:13*

Why call ye me, Lord, Lord, and do not the things which I say? *Luke 6:46*

OPPORTUNITY

The harvest is past, the summer is ended, and we are not saved. *Jer. 8:20*

I must work the works of him that sent me, while it is day: the night cometh, when no man can work.
John 9:4

PARENTS

Honour thy father and thy mother. *Ex. 10:12*

My son, hear the instruction of thy father, and forsake not the law of thy mother. *Prov. 1:8*

Who curseth his father or his mother, his lamp shall be put out in obscure darkness. *Prov. 20:20*

Children, obey your parents in the Lord: for this is right.
Eph. 6:1

PATIENCE

Those that wait upon the Lord, they shall inherit the earth. *Psa. 37:9*

The patient in spirit is better than the proud in spirit. *Eccl. 7:8*

Let us not be weary in well doing: for in due season we shall reap, if we faint not. *Gal. 6:9*

Let us run with patience the race that is set before us. *Heb. 12:1*

PEACE

Let there be no strife, I pray thee, between me and thee . . . for we be brethren. *Gen. 13:8*

They shall beat their swords into plowshares, and their spears into pruninghooks. *Isa. 2:4*

Blessed are the peacemakers: for they shall be called the children of God. *Matt. 5:9*

Let the peace of God rule in your heart. *Col. 3:15*

PERFECTION

Be ye therefore perfect, even as your Father which is in heaven is perfect. *Matt. 5:48*

PERSECUTION

Blessed are they which are persecuted for righteousness' sake: for theirs is the kingdom of heaven. Blessed are ye, when men shall revile you, and persecute you, and shall say all manner of evil against you falsely, for my sake. Rejoice, and be exceeding glad: for great is your reward in heaven: for so persecuted they the prophets which were before you. *Matt. 5:10-12*

PESSIMISM

In much wisdom is much grief; and he that increaseth knowledge increaseth sorrow. *Eccl. 1:18*

There is not a just man upon earth, that doeth good, and sinneth not. *Eccl. 7:20*

PLEASURE

He that loveth pleasure shall be a poor man: he that loveth wine and oil shall not be rich. *Prov. 21:17*

A time to weep, and a time to laugh; a time to mourn, and a time to dance. *Eccl. 3:4*

PLENTY

Give and it shall be given unto you; good measure, pressed down, and shaken together, and running over.
Luke 6:38

POSSESSION

Where your treasure is, there will your heart be also.
Matt. 6:21

What is a man profited, if he shall gain the whole world, and lose his own soul? *Matt. 16:26*

POVERTY

The poor is hated even of his own neighbour: but the rich hath many friends. *Prov. 14:20*

He that hath pity upon the poor lendeth unto the Lord; and that which he hath given will he pay him again.
Prov. 19:17

The rich and poor meet together: the Lord is the maker of them all. *Prov. 22:2*

PRAYER

In the day of my trouble I will call upon thee: for thou wilt answer me. *Psa. 86:7*

When thou prayest, thou shalt not be as the hypocrites are: for they love to pray standing in the synagogues and in the corners of the streets, that they may be seen of men.
Matt. 6:5

Ask, and it shall be given you; seek and ye shall find; knock, and it shall be opened unto you. *Matt. 7:7*

All things, whatsoever ye shall ask in prayer, believing, ye shall receive. *Matt. 21:2*

PRIDE

Every one that is proud in heart is an abomination to the Lord. *Prov. 16:5*

Before destruction the heart of man is haughty, and before honour is humility. *Prov. 18:12*

Whatsoever shall exalt himself shall be abased; and he that humble himself shall be exalted. *Matt. 23:12*

REJOICING

The Lord is my strength and my shield; my heart trusted in him, and I am helped: therefore my heart greatly rejoiceth; and with my song will I praise him.

Psa. 28:7

RELIGION

Fear God, and keep his commandments: for this is the whole duty of man. *Eccl. 12:13*

What doth the Lord require of thee, but to do justly, and to love mercy, and to walk humbly with thy God?

Mic. 6:8

REMORSE

The sacrifices of God are a broken spirit: a broken and a contrite heart, O God, thou wilt not despise.

Psa. 51:17

REPENTANCE

Except ye repent, ye shall all likewise perish.

Luke 13:3

I will arise and go to my father, and will say unto him, Father, I have sinned against heaven, and before thee.

Luke 15:18

God be merciful to me a sinner. *Luke 18:13*

RESOLUTION

As for me and my house, we will serve the Lord.

Josh. 24:15

Watch ye, stand fast in the faith, quit you like men, be strong. *I Cor. 16:13*

RESPONSIBILITY

Every one of us shall give account of himself to God.

Rom. 14:12

RETALIATION

Whosoever shall smite thee on thy right cheek, turn to him the other also. *Matt. 5:39*

Judge not, that ye be not judged. For with what judgment ye judge, ye shall be judged; and with what measure ye mete, it shall be measured to you again. *Matt. 7:1, 2*

REVERENCE

The place whereon thou standest is holy ground.
Ex. 3:5

What doth the Lord thy God require of thee, but to fear the Lord thy God, to walk in all his ways, and to love him, and to serve the Lord thy God with all thy heart and with all thy soul. *Deut. 10:12*

Let all the earth fear the Lord: let all the inhabitants of the world stand in awe of him. *Psa. 33:8*

The fear of the Lord is the beginning of wisdom.
Psa. 111:10

REWARD

The righteous shall inherit the earth. *Psa. 37:29*

Cast thy bread upon the waters: for thou shalt find it after many days. *Eccl. 11:1*

Blessed are they which do hunger and thirst after righteousness: for they shall be filled. Blessed are the merciful: for they shall obtain mercy. Blessed are the pure in heart: for they shall see God. Blessed are the peace-makers: for they shall be called the children of God. Blessed are they which are persecuted for righteousness' sake: for theirs is the kingdom of heaven. *Matt. 5:3-12*

Whosoever shall give you a cup of water to drink in my name . . . verily I say unto you, he shall not lose his reward.
Mark 9:41

Every man shall receive his own reward according to his own labour. *I Cor. 3:8*

Whatsoever a man soweth, that shall he also reap.
Gal. 6:7

SACRIFICE

The sacrifices of God are a broken heart. *Psa. 51:17*

If thou wilt be perfect, go and sell what thou hast, and give to the poor, and thou shalt have treasure in heaven: and come and follow me. *Matt. 19:20*

He that loveth his life shall lose it. *John 12:25*

SADNESS

Heaviness in the heart of man maketh it stoop: but a good word maketh it glad. *Prov. 12:25*

SCRIPTURE

Whosoever heareth these sayings of mine, and doeth them, I will liken him unto a wise man, which built his house upon a rock. *Matt. 7:24*

Blessed are they that hear the word of God and keep it. *Luke 11:28*

SELFISHNESS

Whoso hath this world's good, and seeth his brother have need, and shutteth up his bowels of compassion from him, how dwelleth the love of God in him? *I John 3:17*

SIN

Be sure your sin will find you out. *Num. 32:23*

As he thinketh in his heart, so is he. *Prov. 23:7*

All we like sheep have gone astray; we have turned every one to his own way. *Isa. 53:6*

God be merciful to me a sinner. *Luke 18:13*

The wages of sin is death. *Rom. 6:23*

If we say that we have no sin, we deceive ourselves, and the truth is not in us. *I John 1:8*

STRENGTH

Be strong, and quit yourselves like men. *I Sam. 4:9*

The race is not to the swift, or the battle to the strong. *Eccl. 9:11*

They that wait on the Lord shall renew their strength; they shall mount up with wings as eagles; they shall run, and not be weary; and they shall walk, and not faint. *Isa. 40:31*

TALENT

He gave some, apostles; and some, prophets; and some, evangelists; and some, pastors and teachers.   *Eph. 4:1*

TEMPTATION

Can a man take fire in his bosom, and his clothes not be burned?   *Prov. 6:27*

Be not overcome of evil, but overcome evil with good.
Rom. 12:21

THANKSGIVING

I will praise the name of God with a song, and magnify him with thanksgiving.   *Psa. 69:30*

O give thanks unto the Lord, for he is good, for his mercy endureth for ever.   *Psa. 107:1*

TOLERANCE

Judge not, that ye be not judged.   *Matt. 7:1*
God is no respecter of persons.   *Acts. 10:34*
Speak evil of no man.   *Tit. 3:2*

TROUBLE

Have mercy upon me, O Lord, for I am in trouble.
Psa. 31:9

God is our refuge and strength, a very present help in trouble.   *Psa. 46:1*

TRUTH

The Lord is good; his mercy is everlasting; and his truth endureth to all generations.   *Psa. 100:5*

Let not mercy and truth forsake thee: bind them about thy neck; write them upon the table of thine heart.
Prov. 3:3

UNBELIEF

The fool hath said in his heart, There is no God.
Psa. 14:1

UNDERSTANDING

I have given thee a wise and understanding heart.
I Kin. 3:12

Happy is the man . . . that getteth understanding.
Prov. 3:13

VIGILANCE

Take ye heed, watch and pray: for ye know not when the time is. *Mark 13:33*

Watch ye, stand fast in the faith, quit you like men, be strong. *I Cor. 16:13*

WANT

He that giveth to the poor shall not lack.
Prov. 28:27

Your Father knoweth what things ye have need of, before ye ask him. *Matt. 6:8*

WEALTH

He that trusteth in his riches shall fall. *Prov. 11:28*

Wealth maketh many friends; but the poor is separated from his neighbor. *Prov. 19:4*

Let not the rich man glory in his riches. *Jer. 9:23*

Where your treasure is, there will your heart be also.
Matt. 6:21

It is easier for a camel to go through the eye of a needle, than for a rich man to enter into the kingdom of God.
Matt. 19:24

Ye cannot serve God and mammon. *Luke 16:13*

WISDOM

Behold the fear of the Lord, that is wisdom; and to depart from evil is understanding. *Job 28:28*

A man's wisdom maketh his face to shine. *Eccl. 8:1*

Wisdom is better than strength. *Eccl. 9:16*

WORKS

Let your light so shine before men, that they may see your good works, and glorify your Father which is in heaven. *Matt. 5:16*

Faith, if it hath not works, is dead. *Jas. 2:17*

WORLDLINESS

Take no thought for your life, what ye shall eat, or what ye shall drink; nor yet for your body, what ye shall put on. Is not life more than meat, and the body more than raiment? *Matt. 6:25*

The wisdom of this world is foolishness with God.
I Cor. 3:19

WORSHIP

I was glad when they said unto me, Let us go into the house of the Lord. *Psa. 122:1*

All nations shall come and worship before thee.
Rev. 15:4

ZEAL

Let us not be weary in well doing: for in due season we shall reap, if we faint not. *Gal. 6:9*

CHAPTER IX

AS THEY SAW IT

The greatest luxury of our wealth is that we can afford a considerateness toward other people's feelings and . . . pride and nationality. We're a very considerate nation, and it makes us look hesitant and weak sometimes. It's important to understand just how far you can indulge your considerateness.   *Robert Frost*

A man given to pride is usually proud of the wrong thing.   *Henry Ford*

Provision for others is a fundamental responsibility of human life.   *Woodrow Wilson*

There are but two powers in the world, the sword and the mind. In the long run the sword is always beaten by the mind.   *Napoleon*

If you aspire to the highest place it is no disgrace to stop at the second, or even the third.   *Cicero*

Education makes a people easy to lead, but difficult to drive; easy to govern, but impossible to enslave.
                                            Henry Brougham

A great memory does not make a mind, any more than a dictionary is a piece of literature.

                                         John Henry Newman

Every luxury must be paid for, and everything is a luxury, starting with being in the world. *Cesare Pavese*

You will never stub your toe standing still. The faster you go, the more chance there is of stubbing your toe, but the more chance you have of getting somewhere.

                                          Charles F. Kettering

Leisure may prove to be a curse rather than a blessing, unless education teaches a flippant world that leisure is not a synonym for entertainment.   *William J. Bogan*

Elderly people and those in authority cannot always be relied upon to take enlightened and comprehending views of what they call the indiscretions of youth.

                                          Winston Churchill

Distrust all in whom the impulse to punish is powerful.

                                                Nietzsche

I have always been among those who believed that the greatest freedom of speech was the greatest safety, because if a man is a fool, the best thing to do is to encourage him to advertise the fact by speaking. *Woodrow Wilson*

Security is when I'm very much in love with somebody extraordinary who loves me back. *Shelley Winters*

Baloney is the unvarnished lie laid on so thick you hate it. Blarney is flattery laid on so thick you love it.
Bishop Fulton Sheen

America is a large, friendly dog in a very small room. Every time it wags a tail, it knocks over a chair.
Arnold Toynbee

Success is the reward of anyone who looks for trouble.
Walter Winchell

Epigram: a wisecrack that played Carnegie Hall.
Oscar Levant

An egghead is one who stands firmly on both feet in mid-air on both sides of the issue. *Homer Ferguson*

A bore is a fellow who opens his mouth and puts his feats in it. *Henry Ford*

There is nothing enduring in life for a woman except what she builds in a man's heart. *Judith Anderson*

Jazz will endure just as long as people hear it through their feet instead of their brains. *John Philip Sousa*

A fanatic is one who can't change his mind and won't change the subject. *Winston Churchill*

It is the cause, and not the death, that makes the martyr.
Napoleon

Conceit is God's gift to little men. *Bruce Barton*

Generally speaking, it's easier to get rid of money than to get it. The exception is called Form 1040.
Changing Times

The inimitable virtue of the British Constitution is that it does not exist. *André Maurois*

When you really want anything, it is best not to depend on the efforts of others, but to work for it yourself.
Anon.

Great men think of opportunity, not time. Time is the excuse of feeble and puzzled spirits. *Disraeli*

In an assembly, the simplest way to stop the transacting of business and split the ranks is to appeal to the principle.
Jacques Barzun

Leadership appears to be the art of getting others to want to do something you are convinced should be done.
Vance Packard

Variety is the spice of life, but it takes monotony to finance it.
Arnold Glasow

People hardly ever make use of the freedom they have, for example, freedom of thought; instead they demand freedom of speech as a compensation.
Kierkegaard

Experience is very valuable. It keeps a man who makes the same mistake twice from admitting it the third time.
Brook Benton

It is not who is right, but what is right, that is of importance.
Thomas Huxley

The cow jumped over the moon. Now Jr. wants to know whether it was planned that way all along or something went wrong with the telemetry.
Changing Times

A liberal is a man too broadminded to take his own side in a quarrel.

Faith is knowing there is an ocean because you have seen a brook.
William A. Ward

Good breeding consists in concealing how much we think of ourselves and how little we think of the other person.
Mark Twain

Every new idea has something of the pain and peril of childbirth about it.
Samuel Butler

The first thing to turn green in the spring is the Christmas jewelry.
Kin Hubbard

The hardest thing for a husband to do when he brings home the bacon is to salt a little away.
Alex Dreier

Gossip is the art of saying nothing in a way that leaves practically nothing unsaid.
Walter Winchell

At no time in the history of the world have so many people had so much; and in a way this is frightening. I suppose this comes from something my mother dinned into my head night and day: "It's bad when things are too good."
Harry Golden

If A equals success, then the formula is A equals X plus Y plus Z. X is work, Y is play and Z is keep your mouth shut. *Albert Einstein*

Optimism is a mania for declaring that all is well when things are going badly. *Voltaire*

Greatness, in the last analysis, is largely bravery — courage in escaping from old ideas and old standards and respectable ways of doing things. This is one of the chief elements in what we vaguely call capacity.
James Harvey Robinson

Be wiser than other people if you can, but do not tell them so. *Lord Chesterfield*

I am not young enough to know everything.
James M. Barrie

When I hear somebody sigh that "Life is hard," I am always tempted to ask, "Compared to what?"
Sydney Harris

Some people would not hesitate to drive up to the gate of heaven and honk. *John Andrew Holmes*

Genius may have its limitations, but stupidity is not thus handicapped. *Elbert Hubbard*

War hath no fury like a noncombatant.
Charles Edward Montague

More erroneous conclusions are due to lack of information, than to errors of judgment. *Louis Brandeis*

One can never pay in gratitude; one can only pay "in mind" somewhere else in life.
Anne Morrow Lindbergh

Behold the turtle. He makes progress only when he sticks his neck out. *James Bryant Conant*

The minds of men are full of shadows and reflections of things they cannot grasp. *Robert M. Hutchins*

It is preoccupation with possessions, more than anything else, that prevents men from living freely and nobly.
Bertrand Russell

Smart people speak from experience. Smarter people, from experience, don't speak. *Paul Gibson*

No path of flowers leads to glory.
Jean de la Fontaine

Nature didn't make us perfect, so she did the next best thing. She made us blind to our own faults.   *Anon.*

Great tranquillity of heart is his who cares for neither praise nor blame.   *Thomas a Kempis*

The next forty years of life give us the text; the next thirty supply the commentary on it.
Arthur Schopenhauer

Necessity is the mother of "taking chances."
Mark Twain

Fashion is that by which the fantastic becomes for a moment universal.   *Oscar Wilde*

No man really becomes a fool until he stops asking questions.   *Charles P. Steinmetz*

Never speak to me about summer; summer has no charms for me. I look forward anxiously to the return of bad weather and blazing fires.   *Sydney Smith*

There are no warlike peoples — just warlike leaders.
Ralph J. Bunche

The only birds that talk are parrots, and they don't fly very high.   *Wilbur Wright*

You will do the greatest service to the state if you shall raise, not the roofs of the houses, but the souls of the citizens; for it is better that great souls should dwell in small houses rather than for mean slaves to lurk in great houses.   *Epictetus*

There is nothing more tragic in life than the utter impossibility of changing what you have done.
John Galsworthy

To be able to fill leisure intelligently is the last product of civilization.   *Bertrand Russell*

A man's worst difficulties begin when he is able to do as he likes.   *T. H. Huxley*

My idea of an agreeable person is a person who agrees with me.   *Benjamin Disraeli*

Peace is not absence of war, it is a virtue, a state of mind, a disposition for benevolence, confidence, justice.
Spinoza

An appeaser is one who feeds a crocodile — hoping it will eat him last.   *Winston Churchill*

A long dispute means that both parties are wrong.
Voltaire

What is the difference between a taxidermist and a tax collector? The taxidermist takes only your skin.
Mark Twain

It is a funny thing about life — if you refuse to accept anything but the very best you very often get it.
W. Somerset Maugham

To be ignorant of the lives of the most celebrated men of antiquity is to continue in a state of childhood all our days.
Plutarch

The world must learn to work together, or finally it will not work at all.
Dwight D. Eisenhower

The men of the past had convictions, while we moderns have only opinions.
Heinrich Heine

Whatever America hopes to bring to pass in this world must first come to pass in the heart of America.
Dwight D. Eisenhower

A thick skin is a gift from God.   *Konrad Adenauer*

When speculation has done its worst, two and two still make four.
Samuel Johnson

The only failure which lacks dignity is the failure to try.
Malcolm F. MacNeil

It has been said that absolute power corrupts absolutely, but may it not be truer to say that to be absolutely powerful a man must first corrupt himself?   *Terence Rattigan*

Censure is the tax a man pays to the public for being eminent.
Jonathan Swift

Procrastination is the art of keeping up with yesterday.
Don Marquis

One must be a god to be able to tell successes from failures without making a mistake.   *Chekhov*

Man is a gregarious animal, and much more so in his mind than in his body. He may like to go alone for a walk, but he hates to stand alone in his opinions.   *Santayana*

Marriage is three parts love and seven parts forgiveness of sins.
Langdon Mitchell

It is when we all play safe that we create a world of utmost insecurity.
Dag Hammarskjold

Too few have the courage of my convictions.
Robert M. Hutchins

Time is a breedy creature: The minutes propagate hours, the hours beget days, the days raise huge families of months, and before we know it we are crowded out of this sweet life by mere surplus of time's offspring.
Christopher Morley

He that falls in love with himself will have no rivals.
Benjamin Franklin

It pays to be honest, but it's beginning to look like the rewards are falling far short of what it costs to live.
Kin Hubbard

The public does not always know what it wants, and . . . it is not always wise to take it at its word.
Francis Wayland

Unless man has the wit and the grit to build his civilization on something better than material power, it is surely idle to talk of plans for a stable peace.
Francis B. Sayre

The only people who achieve much are those who want knowledge so badly that they seek it while the conditions are still unfavorable. Favorable conditions never come.
C. S. Lewis

The circus is the only fun you can buy that's good for you.
Ernest Hemingway

Acquaintance: A degree of friendship called slight when its object is poor and obscure, and intimate when he is rich and famous.
Ambrose Bierce

Men of thought should have nothing to do with action.
Oscar Wilde

Perfection seems to be nothing more than a complete adaptation to the environment; but the environment is constantly changing, so perfection can never be more than transitory.
W. Somerset Maugham

The undisciplined mind is far better adapted to the confused world in which we live today than the streamlined mind.
James Thurber

By trying we can easily learn to endure adversity. Another man's, I mean.
Mark Twain

You can tell the ideals of a nation by its advertisements.
Norman Douglas

When I had looked at the lights of Broadway by night, I said to my American friends: "What a glorious garden of wonders this would be, to any one who was lucky enough to be unable to read." *G. K. Chesterton*

The only thing to do with good advice is to pass it on. It is never of any use to oneself. *Oscar Wilde*

Amusement is the happiness of those that cannot think.
Alexander Pope

I never read a book before reviewing it. It prejudices one so! *Sydney Smith*

Sartor Resartus is simply unreadable, and for me that always sort of spoils a book. *Will Cuppy*

I not only use all the brains I have, but all I can borrow.
Woodrow Wilson

A bee is never as busy as it seems; it's just that it can't buzz any slower. *Kin Hubbard*

A child thinks twenty shillings and twenty years can scarce ever be spent. *Benjamin Franklin*

City life: Millions of people being lonesome together.
Henry David Thoreau

Cynicism is intellectual dandyism. *George Meredith*

A cynic is just a man who found out when he was about ten that there wasn't any Santa Claus, and he's still upset.
James Gould Cozzens

It is a mistake to look too far ahead. Only one link in the chain of destiny can be handled at a time.
Winston S. Churchill

The trouble with the dictionary is that you have to know how a word is spelled before you can look it up to see how it is spelled. *Will Cuppy*

Digestion is the great secret of life. *Sydney Smith*

A dog teaches a boy fidelity, perseverance, and to turn about three times before lying down.
Robert Benchley

The happiest time in any man's life is when he is in red-hot pursuit of a dollar with a reasonable prospect of overtaking it. *Josh Billings*

When in doubt, tell the truth.   *Mark Twain*

A great many people use faulty English without knowing it. Ain't you?   *Robert Benchley*

Etiquette means behaving yourself a little better than is absolutely essential.   *Will Cuppy*

Few things are harder to put up with than the annoyance of a good example.   *Mark Twain*

Experience is the name everyone gives to their mistakes.
   Oscar Wilde

We learn from experience that men never learn anything from experience.   *George Bernard Shaw*

A family is a unit composed not only of children, but of men, women, an occasional animal, and the common cold.
   Ogden Nash

Even if a farmer intends to loaf, he gets up in time to get an early start.   *E. W. Howe*

Most people enjoy the inferiority of their best friends.
   Lord Chesterfield

Prosperity makes few friends.   *Vauvenargues*

It is almost impossible to remember how tragic a place the world is when one is playing golf.   *Robert Lynd*

When a man buys a new hat, he wants one just like the one he has had before. But a woman isn't that way.
   E. W. Howe

An idea that is not dangerous is unworthy of being called an idea at all.   *Oscar Wilde*

Few women and fewer men have enough character to be idle.   *E. V. Lucas*

I do not mind lying, but I hate inaccuracy.
   Samuel Butler

Man sees your actions, but God your motives.
   Thomas a Kempis

Classic music is the kind that we keep thinking will turn into a tune.   *Kin Hubbard*

We do not know a nation until we know its pleasures of life, just as we do not know a man until we know how he spends his leisure.   *Lin Yutang*

The worst sensation I know of is getting up at night and stepping on a toy train of cars.   *Kin Hubbard*

I was gratified to be able to answer promptly and I did. I said I didn't know. *Mark Twain*

Unhappiness is in not knowing what we want and killing ourselves to get it. *Don Herold*

No question is so difficult to answer as that to which the answer is obvious. *George Bernard Shaw*

The greatest compensation of old age is its freedom of spirit . . . Another compensation is that it liberates you from envy, hatred, and malice. *W. Somerset Maugham*

There is nothing more beautiful in this world than a healthy wise old man. *Lin Yutang*

Have a place for everything and keep the thing somewhere else; this is not advice, it is merely custom. *Mark Twain*

We all have strength enough to endure the misfortunes of others. *La Rochefoucauld*

The worst jolt most of us ever get is when we fall back on our own resources. *Kin Hubbard*

To bring up a child in the way he should go, travel that way yourself once in a while. *Josh Billings*

He that can have patience can have what he will. *Benjamin Franklin*

All are lunatics, but he who can analyze his delusions is called a philosopher. *Ambrose Bierce*

A practical man is a man who practices the errors of his forefathers. *Benjamin Disraeli*

I don't like principles. I prefer prejudices. *Oscar Wilde*

Nowadays people know the price of everything and the value of nothing. *Oscar Wilde*

Principles have no real force except when one is well fed. *Mark Twain*

When a fellow says, "It ain't the money, but the principle of the thing," it's the money. *Kin Hubbard*

All progress is based upon a universal desire on the part of every organism to live beyond its income. *Samuel Butler*

Punctuality is the thief of time. *Oscar Wilde*

Ignorant men raise questions that wise men answered a thousand years ago. *Goethe*

The "silly question" is the first intimation of some totally new development. *Alfred North Whitehead*

At the Day of Judgment we shall not be asked what we have read but what we have done. *Thomas a Kempis*

The hardest thing is writing a recommendation for someone we know. *Kin Hubbard*

Nothing so needs reforming as other people's habits. *Mark Twain*

If you destroy a free market you create a black market. If you have ten thousand regulations you destroy all respect for the law. *Winston S. Churchill*

Short of genius, a rich man cannot imagine poverty. *Charles Peguy*

Rudeness is the weak man's imitation of strength. *Eric Hoffer*

Much may be made of a Scotchman if he be caught young. *Samuel Johnson*

Spiritual life and secure life do not go together. To save oneself one must struggle and take risks. *Ignazio Silone*

Seldom is anyone so spiritual as to strip himself entirely of self-love. *Thomas a Kempis*

Self-sacrifice enables us to sacrifice other people without blushing. *George Bernard Shaw*

Selfishness is not living as one wishes to live, it is asking others to live as one wishes to live. *Oscar Wilde*

I believe in the discipline of silence and could talk for hours about it. *George Bernard Shaw*

It ain't a bad plan to keep still occasionally even when you know what you are talking about. *Kin Hubbard*

Of all the substitutes, a substitute speaker is the worst. *Kin Hubbard*

The hardest thing to stop is a temporary chairman. *Kin Hubbard*

It is better to be stupid like everybody than clever like none. *Anatole France*

There is always something about your success that displeases even your best friends. *Oscar Wilde*

If at first you do succeed, don't take any more chances. *Kin Hubbard*

No man would listen to you talk if he didn't know it was his turn next. *E. W. Howe*

If you tell the truth, you don't have to remember anything. *Mark Twain*

Nothing really belongs to us but time, which even he has who has nothing else. *Baltasar Gracian*

We all find time to do what we really want to do. *William Feather*

In America there are two classes of travel — first class, and with children. *Robert Benchley*

But men do not seek the truth. It is the truth that pursues men who run away and will not look around. *Lincoln Steffens*

Good breeding consists in concealing how much we think of ourselves and how little we think of the other person. *Mark Twain*

Slowly but surely humanity realizes the dreams of the wise. *Anatole France*

A woman who is confuted is never convinced. *John Churton Collins*

Words are the clothes that thoughts wear — only the clothes. *Samuel Butler*

I do not like work even when another person does it. *Mark Twain*

Work is love made visible. *Kahlil Gibran*

Man draws the nearer to God as he withdraws further from the consolations of this world. *Thomas a Kempis*

The world will, in the end, follow only those who have despised as well as served it. *Samuel Butler*

The world ain't getting no worse; we've only got better facilities. *Kin Hubbard*

I remember my youth and the feeling that will never come back any more — the feeling that I could last forever, outlast the sea, and all men. *Joseph Conrad*

INDEX